# Calling Him Trusted

## Developing a Relationship with Jesus while Living with Complex Trauma Disorder

### Evangeline North

# Contents

# Dedication

This book is dedicated to my God. I wrote it because you asked me to. Your love which has changed my life is unfathomable and so good. Thank you for loving me.

To my children because the only truly good thing I can leave you in this life, the only thing I hope to pass down is a relationship with Jesus. I love you.

To my husband because loving you has been worth it.

To the Pederson family, thank you for saying yes to God's ask. My life and my capacity to love and be loved have forever been changed. I'm grateful to call you family. I love you.

To my mom, thank you for choosing to love Jesus and for doing the hard work of staying clean. I'm grateful to have a relationship with you. I love you.

To my siblings, those who I grew up with, my hope and desire is that one day you will know the joy and the hope that comes from having a loving relationship with Jesus.

# Preface

My purpose and hope in writing this book are three-fold. First, that my story and journey in trusting God will provide anchors for the readers living with Complex Trauma Disorder (CTD) so they can journey with a clear and more defined picture of the God they are searching for. Second, I hope to give readers who do not live with CTD a glimpse into the types of experiences that cause people to develop this disorder, an understanding of the types of things people with this disorder have to process to maintain relationships, and the importance of their role as friends or family members. And third, I hope that the church, specifically pastors and leaders within the church, read this book to understand the importance of teaching and preaching *Shalom* so that those with CTD have a safe place to worship and be in community.

He is love, they said. He is good, they said. You can trust Him, they said. I searched for this God they described while living undiagnosed and without an understanding of CTD. I felt like a blind woman navigating an unknown room, searching for God while listening to the voices describing Him. But it was so dark, and as I searched, I longed to trust Him without fear of betrayal, abuse, or abandonment; without fear that the God at the end of my search might be filled with hate and anger and rage.

I explain CTD and its effects on me in this way: as a child, while living through consistent abusive situations by my primary caregivers, my brain developed for survival, creating tactics and strategies for safety. Throughout my day I lived in a state of hypervigilance, constantly sizing people up based on safety, planning my escape route, scanning my environment, reading body language and tone of voice, and examining facial expressions. After having my first child, the intensity of my heightened hypervigilance became difficult to manage, which is what led to my diagnosis.

A primary and distinctive characteristic of CTD as it affects me is a lack of trust within all my relationships. Therefore, trusting God provides me with an anchor that allows me to stabilize myself while navigating other relationships.

God's character is a focus in this book because trusting Him is anchored in finding safety in His character. I find relationship with God imperative for maintaining my mental health and for connecting and attaching to others who constantly fail at being safe enough for me. Anchoring to one trusted, never-changing relationship with God has given me a safe place to rest and regroup in order to stay committed to my friendships, my marriage, and my children. So, to you, who have or may have CTD, I hope this book is helpful for establishing or deepening your relationship with God so that you have someone to anchor to while navigating human relationships.

Before we dive deeper, it is important that CTD is understood thoroughly, at least by definition. So, to make sure we are on the same page regarding the identity of CTD, here are three definitions.

1- As defined by Complextrauma.org:

COMPLEX TRAUMA IS DISTINCT FROM THE MULTITUDE OF OTHER TERMS THAT EXIST TO DESCRIBE TYPES OF TRAUMA EXPOSURE OR MANIFESTATIONS OF POSTTRAUMATIC DISTURBANCE.

COMPLEX TRAUMA IS DEFINED AS THE EXPOSURE TO MULTIPLE, OFTEN INTERRELATED FORMS OF TRAUMATIC EXPERIENCES AND THE DIFFICULTIES THAT ARISE AS A RESULT OF ADAPTING TO OR SURVIVING THESE EXPERIENCES.

THE ADVERSE EXPERIENCES ENCAPSULATED BY COMPLEX TRAUMA TYPICALLY BEGIN IN EARLY CHILDHOOD, ARE LONGSTANDING OR RECURRENT, AND ARE INFLICTED BY OTHERS. MOST OFTEN THEY ARE PERPETRATED WITHIN A PERSON'S FORMATIVE ATTACHMENT RELATIONSHIPS. SOMETIMES THEY ARE COMPOUNDED BY PATTERNS OF RISK AND DYSFUNCTION AFFLICTING GENERATIONS OF FAMILIES. FREQUENTLY, THEY INTERSECT WITH STRUCTURAL AND INSTITUTIONAL FORMS OF VIOLENCE AND OPPRESSION THAT BESET CERTAIN PEOPLES AND COMMUNITIES, PARTICULARLY THOSE HOLDING MINORITY STATUS WITHIN A GIVEN SOCIETY.

THE OUTCOMES ASSOCIATED WITH COMPLEX TRAUMA SPAN A WIDE RANGE OF PSYCHIATRIC DIAGNOSES AND MISDIAGNOSES, FUNCTIONAL IMPAIRMENTS, AND EVOLVING EDUCATIONAL, VOCATIONAL, RELATIONAL, AND HEALTH PROBLEMS.

2 - As defined by The National Child Traumatic Stress Network:

COMPLEX TRAUMA DESCRIBES BOTH CHILDREN'S EXPOSURE TO
MULTIPLE TRAUMATIC EVENTS—OFTEN OF AN INVASIVE, INTER-
PERSONAL NATURE—AND THE WIDE-RANGING, LONG-TERM EF-
FECTS OF THIS EXPOSURE. THESE EVENTS ARE SEVERE AND PER-
VASIVE, SUCH AS ABUSE OR PROFOUND NEGLECT. THEY USUALLY
OCCUR EARLY IN LIFE AND CAN DISRUPT MANY ASPECTS OF THE
CHILD'S DEVELOPMENT AND THE FORMATION OF A SENSE OF SELF.
SINCE THESE EVENTS OFTEN OCCUR WITH A CAREGIVER, THEY IN-
TERFERE WITH THE CHILD'S ABILITY TO FORM A SECURE ATTACH-
MENT. MANY ASPECTS OF A CHILD'S HEALTHY PHYSICAL AND MEN-
TAL DEVELOPMENT RELY ON THIS PRIMARY SOURCE OF SAFETY AND
STABILITY.

Although Complex Trauma Disorder is not yet an official diagnosis
in the United States, the World Health Organization has included the
diagnosis and its diagnostic criteria under the diagnostic label Complex
Post-Traumatic Stress Disorder (C-PTSD) in the International Statisti-
cal Classification of Diseases and Related Health Problems (ICD-11).

3 – As defined in the ICD-11:

COMPLEX POST TRAUMATIC STRESS DISORDER (C-PTSD) IS A DIS-
ORDER THAT MAY DEVELOP FOLLOWING EXPOSURE TO AN EVENT
OR SERIES OF EVENTS OF AN EXTREMELY THREATENING OR HORRIF-
IC NATURE, MOST COMMONLY PROLONGED OR REPETITIVE EVENTS
FROM WHICH ESCAPE IS DIFFICULT OR IMPOSSIBLE (E.G. TOR-

TURE, SLAVERY, GENOCIDE CAMPAIGNS, PROLONGED DOMESTIC VI-
OLENCE, REPEATED CHILDHOOD SEXUAL OR PHYSICAL ABUSE). ALL
DIAGNOSTIC REQUIREMENTS FOR PTSD ARE MET. IN ADDITION,
COMPLEX PTSD IS CHARACTERIZED BY SEVERE AND PERSISTENT 1)
PROBLEMS IN AFFECT REGULATION; 2) BELIEFS ABOUT ONESELF AS
DIMINISHED, DEFEATED, OR WORTHLESS, ACCOMPANIED BY FEEL-
INGS OF SHAME, GUILT, OR FAILURE RELATED TO THE TRAUMATIC
EVENT; AND 3) DIFFICULTIES IN SUSTAINING RELATIONSHIPS AND IN
FEELING CLOSE TO OTHERS. THESE SYMPTOMS CAUSE SIGNIFICANT
IMPAIRMENT IN PERSONAL, FAMILY, SOCIAL, EDUCATIONAL, OCCU-
PATIONAL, OR OTHER IMPORTANT AREAS OF FUNCTIONING.

CTD is linked to dissociation and memory loss. I share in this book what I do remember. However, please be aware that my memories come from my perspective and the emotion felt in those places and moments of fear. The clearest way I can explain this is through an experience I recently had with our son.

Our son, who is adopted, asked if he could see the home he grew up in using Google Earth. Although he was very young when he was in that home, he was still, after all these years, able to describe in detail the experiences and activities that went on in his childhood home that were consistent with the layout of his home as I remember it and was shown on Google Earth. However, when we sat down to look at his home on Google Earth his response to viewing his home was confusion.

After I had pulled up the address and moved the yellow man icon to the front of his childhood home, I waited for a reaction. When there was no reaction, I looked back at his face, which was covered in anticipation, as if he was waiting for his house to appear. Eventually, I simply said, "This is your old house." To which he responded, "No, that's not my house."

To help him, I used the yellow man icon within the program to share multiple views of the house, while I recalled details he had previously shared with me to help him make the connections. When he still looked confused, I asked him what he was thinking and he said, "That house doesn't match the house that's in my head." You see, the house we were looking at was located on a clean property. It was painted in a light color and the paint job was still good. When I asked him what the picture of his house looked like in his head, he described a house that was dark with trash on the ground, broken boards on the front of the house, a roof that was falling in, and paint that was peeling.

Several months earlier we had walked past an abandoned house that looked similar to his description. While walking past this house he came very close to me, grabbed my hand, and in a shaky voice said, "That house reminds me of my old one." Sometimes the way we felt in a place changes our perspective and memory of that place. My son remembers a house that was scary, one that felt unsafe and unlivable.

I say all of this to explain that this book is written from my perspective, from feelings of helplessness and fear and memories of relationships that were dilapidated and a heart that was uninhabitable. My seven brothers and sisters and I may all remember the same beatings in different ways, with different emphases having different impacts. Therefore, these memories, descriptions of events, and the impacts of them tell only my story, from my perspective.

If you have CTD, I hope that by reading this book you feel less alone, more hopeful, and more willing to consider a relationship with God who sees you, loves you, and values you in order for you to have someone you trust to anchor to.

# Trigger Warning

The material in this book may be triggering for some readers. If you have CTD or have concerns that you might be triggered by my personal stories, please consider moving gently past the excerpts recalling my experiences.

# Disclaimer

This book is a work of non-fiction, based on the life, experiences, and recollections of the author. The author has taken reasonable steps to provide accurate information. However, certain liberties have been taken to protect the privacy of individuals and to assist in the narrative flow. Names, identifying characteristics, and details have been changed or fictionalized to protect privacy. Some events have been altered or compressed for the sake of brevity and clarity, and some dialogue has been reimagined or paraphrased to better fit the narrative.

# Part I

# Ransom Her

Brand love on her heart so that she remembers your thoughts about her when the angry words and the all-encompassing voices of self-hate and rage and manipulation weaken her resolve.

Seek her so that what's left of her gentleness will sense you, love, as she reaches for her self-mutilation tool.

Save her so she remembers the softness of herself, her worth, her value, her beauty.

Brand *love* on her heart...

...and ransom her.

# Chapter One

## God, Who Sees Me

*Can you make something from the wreckage? Would you take this heart and make it whole again?* - Bryan Fowler, Keith Everette Smith, Micah Darrel Kuiper and Tasha Layton, *Into the Sea (It's Gonna Be Okay)*

The living room was black when I heard the car pull into the driveway. Although I didn't know the time of night, I knew it was late enough that my brother and I were supposed to be asleep. My dad stood at the door waiting for it to open. Holding my breath and narrowing my eyes so he wouldn't notice that I was awake, I could see that he was standing in a position where whoever was outside would not be able to see his body. But my Aunt Danae, the woman he lived with and was sleeping with, who would unlock and open the door, would be greeted with my dad's threatening face as a prelude and an announcement for what was to come. I heard the car door shut. I heard the key turn in the doorknob. I watched as the door opened. After her eyes met his, she put a smile on her face, turned to the car that had just dropped her off, and waved; I heard it pull away.

My dad only allowed the door to open a few inches, which forced Danae to have to push and squeeze her way through the space between the door and the door jam to get into the house. In my five-year-old body, I felt the meanness of this. It was demeaning and cruel to require her to push and squeeze herself through a small opening to get into a house that would hide her beating.

Once she was in, he closed and locked the door behind her. I can still remember the feeling of watching the door lock. It was a feeling that would visit me over the next thirteen years: degrading submission, accompanied by a feeling that there was no escape. A few whispered exchanges took place, and then I watched as Danae willingly followed him to their bedroom. I heard their door shut and then silence.

The silence was eventually broken by her screams, "No, no, no, Dez, please, noooo." We could hear her begging him to put his machete away. My body held a stiffness that felt like my bones had been fused together as I listened to her blame her tardiness on her stupidity; the begging always to follow. She tried with her most sincere pleading to get him to believe that the man in the car with the others was just a friend of another woman; again, the begging.

I lay on the living room floor with my head on a pillow partially covered by a blanket. My fear kept me from moving. I wanted to breathe normally, to scream, to weep, to run for help. Instead, I made the effort to take breaths in shallow, stable rhythms to not be noticed. My younger brother lay next to me under the same blanket, and although I was not yet old enough for kindergarten, with his eyes open, staring at my face, and his body unmoving he asked, "What do we do?" At five, my response was, "If they come out of the bedroom, keep your eyes closed and pretend you're sleeping."

I'm not sure how much time passed, but eventually, their door opened and it was silent, then the back door opened. A while later the back door shut and then their bedroom door shut. I didn't hear anything else the rest of the night. I lay there awake with my eyes closed until my body, against my will, gave way and I fell asleep.

I woke up the next morning to a conversation Danae was having on the phone. Still unmoving, I listened as she told the person on the other end of the phone how my dad had stripped her naked, taken her to the backyard, tied her to a chair, and left her there all night as punishment.

I spent so many years angry with God. Angry that God saw five-year-old me lying on that living room floor without saving me, my brother, or Danae. Angry that He created me knowing the kind of childhood I would have, angry that he seemed to do nothing or care at all.

In college, when I started processing some of my trauma I would sit with friends and cry. I'd hold my middle finger toward the sky and say, "I hate you." In contempt and with accusation, I'd demand, "How can you (God) be good? You saw and you did nothing." There were times I approached God in a spirit of grief to tell Him I thought his decision-making and timing were cruel.

Despite the anger and contempt, those moments were some of my first moments of intimacy with God. Showing Him my anger, my hurt and my sadness were vulnerable moments between the two of us. I could have easily denied Him the relationship with me, but had I avoided the conversation altogether, He never would have had the opportunity to respond.

After college, I continued to seek God with all my contempt and anger. I ran across a name of God that I had never heard before El Roi. El Roi means "God who sees me." This name that describes God is used only once in the Bible by an Egyptian slave named Hagar. Hagar was abused by her owner Sarai, and when the abuse became too much, Hagar fled. God saw, met with her, and gave her direction, instruction, and hope. Genesis chapter sixteen tells the story:

NOW SARAI, ABRAM'S WIFE, HAD BORNE HIM NO CHILDREN. SHE HAD A FEMALE EGYPTIAN SERVANT WHOSE NAME WAS HAGAR. AND SARAI SAID TO ABRAM, "BEHOLD NOW, THE LORD HAS PREVENTED ME FROM BEARING CHILDREN. GO INTO MY SERVANT; IT MAY BE THAT I SHALL OBTAIN CHILDREN BY HER." AND ABRAM LISTENED TO THE VOICE OF SARAI. SO, AFTER ABRAM HAD LIVED TEN YEARS IN THE LAND OF CANAAN, SARAI, ABRAM'S WIFE, TOOK HAGAR THE EGYPTIAN, HER SERVANT, AND GAVE HER TO ABRAM HER HUSBAND AS A WIFE. AND HE WENT INTO HAGAR, AND SHE CONCEIVED. AND WHEN SHE SAW THAT SHE HAD CONCEIVED, SHE LOOKED WITH CONTEMPT ON HER MISTRESS. AND SARAI SAID TO ABRAM, "MAY THE WRONG DONE TO ME BE ON YOU! I GAVE MY SERVANT TO YOUR EMBRACE, AND WHEN SHE SAW THAT SHE HAD CONCEIVED, SHE LOOKED ON ME WITH CONTEMPT. MAY THE LORD JUDGE BETWEEN YOU AND ME!" BUT ABRAM SAID TO SARAI, "BEHOLD, YOUR SER- VANT IS IN YOUR POWER; DO TO HER AS YOU PLEASE." THEN SARAI DEALT HARSHLY WITH HER, AND SHE (HAGAR) FLED FROM HER. (GENESIS 16: 1-6, ESV)

It took several times reading this passage for the true realities of this situation to sink in. Hagar had been living as a servant to Sarai, beneath her in slave-like submission, when all of a sudden in owner-slave fashion, Hagar is told she will become Abram's wife and is to sleep with him. This resulted in Hagar getting pregnant. Hagar then sees Sarai differently, looking at Sarai "with contempt." In other words, Hagar for the first time is in a position to see Sarai as lower than herself and Sarai doesn't like it. To regain control of the situation Sarai becomes an abuser.

Sarai is the one who thought up the scheme, orchestrated the marriage, had the idea to get Hagar pregnant, and was the one responsible for Hagar's status change. However, when things don't turn out the way Sarai expects, she goes into manipulation and control mode. She approaches Abram to blame him for her "misfortune" and then threatens him to have the Lord judge him. Abram, having no boundaries, then participates in the abuse by giving Sarai free reign on how she treats Hagar. The Bible says that Sarai treated Hagar "harshly."

Originally, when I read the word "harshly" it didn't alert me to the idea that it could possibly be abuse, neglect, or otherwise something horrible. However, it must have been horrible. Hagar, pregnant and living in ancient Egypt, would not have fled into the wilderness with nothing unless the treatment was unbearable and maybe even unlivable. A woman, in those days, would not have run into the wilderness unless her situation felt hopeless.

Genesis 16 finishes like this:

THE ANGEL OF THE LORD FOUND HER (HAGAR) BY A SPRING OF WATER IN THE WILDERNESS, THE SPRING ON THE WAY TO SHUR. AND HE SAID, "HAGAR, SERVANT OF SARAI, WHERE HAVE YOU COME FROM AND WHERE ARE YOU GOING?" SHE SAID, "I AM FLEEING FROM MY MISTRESS SARAI," THE ANGEL OF THE LORD SAID TO HER, "RE-TURN TO YOUR MISTRESS AND SUBMIT TO HER." THE ANGEL OF THE LORD ALSO SAID TO HER, "I WILL SURELY MULTIPLY YOUR OFF-SPRING SO THAT THEY CANNOT BE NUMBERED FOR MULTITUDE." AND THE ANGEL OF THE LORD SAID TO HER, "BEHOLD, YOU ARE PREGNANT AND SHALL BEAR A SON. YOU SHALL CALL HIS NAME

ISHMAEL BECAUSE THE LORD HAS LISTENED TO YOUR AFFLICTION. HE SHALL BE A WILD DONKEY OF A MAN, HIS HAND AGAINST EVERY-ONE AND EVERYONE'S HAND AGAINST HIM, AND HE SHALL DWELL OVER AGAINST ALL HIS KINGSMEN." SO, SHE CALLED THE NAME OF THE LORD WHO SPOKE TO HER, "YOU ARE A GOD OF SEEING." FOR SHE SAID, "TRULY HERE I HAVE SEEN HIM WHO LOOKS AFTER ME." THEREFORE, THE WELL WAS CALLED BEER-LAHAI-ROI; IT LIES BETWEEN KADESH AND BERED. AND HAGAR BORE ABRAM A SON, AND ABRAM CALLED THE NAME OF HIS SON, WHOM HAGAR BORE, ISHMAEL, ABRAM WAS EIGHTY-SIX YEARS OLD WHEN HAGAR BORE ISHMAEL TO ABRAM. (GENESIS 16:7-15, ESV)

After reading this passage, I felt push-back from God in response to my accusations against him. I heard him saying, "I saw Hagar and because I saw, I knew how to take care of her." God gave her a son and promised to multiply her descendants, making her worth, at that time, insurmountable. God sent an angel to meet her at the water to tell her she is seen.

It wasn't until reading this passage that I was able to question myself, to consider that maybe God could be good? Maybe He does care? What if, instead of "You, (God) saw and did nothing," the reality was actually, "You, (God) saw and so you know all that needs to be mended, where to start, and how to love me?"

Reader, He sees you. He knows every hurt, every moment of fear, each demeaning act and moral shift you had to make to stay safe, and in some cases, *alive*. Because He sees you, because He is El Roi, He knows how to heal the parts of you that you feel are unmendable, bring to light the secrets you haven't told, and overcome the lies you believe. He knows how to restore what you think you'll never get back. He promises to be with you each step as you choose to move forward. Like Hagar, when you aren't sure where you're going, He will give you direction, instruction, and hope.

> "Be strong and courageous. Do not be afraid or terrified because of them, for the LORD your God goes with you; he will never leave you nor forsake you." (Deuteronomy 31:6, NIV)

# Ponder

Consider pondering the following questions. To be gentle with yourself, I suggest pondering one set of questions a day, being as honest as possible. Have empathy for yourself in this process.

How does it feel to learn that in your moments of abuse or neglect, God saw you, that He was there with you while you endured your suffering?

What are some things you accuse God of?

Do you accuse and silence God? If so, how do you silence Him? Do you refuse to read the Bible, refuse to pray, or refuse, because of God, to go to church? Do you intentionally keep a distance between you and God in order to not give Him a relationship with you?

Do you accuse God and allow Him to respond? If so, how do you allow Him to respond? Do you listen? If so, how? Do you read the Bible? Are you able to be in the presence of God and remain vulnerable or do you find that when praying or learning about God you feel protective of yourself, maybe ready to argue or defend yourself? Why?

Do you believe God saw what happened to you and that He has a plan to redeem, restore and take care of you? Have you seen some of these things happen already? If so, how?

While looking back on your abuse are you able to see God's hand in your situation? Maybe He provided someone or something at just the right time? Or maybe He protected you from a worse situation?

Make a list of the parts of you that you feel are unmendable. Consider asking God to help mend them.

# Chapter Two

## My Anchor

*I have told you these things, so that in me you may have peace. In this world you will have trouble. But take heart! I have overcome the world. -* John 16:33, NIV

When I was two years old, my mom found Danae, (her younger sister), and my dad having an affair. My mom, along with the rest of my family, called it an affair. They villainized Danae and used their shared disgust for her as a common bond. When I listened to my family talk of the matter, my dad's name was never used with contempt. They never blamed him, never held him responsible for any actions in the matter, at least not in front of me. It was clear, though, that Danae was, at the least, not liked amongst family members and, at the most, despised. Danae was around sixteen at the time and my dad was over twenty.

It wasn't until I was sixteen that I questioned my family's thoughts on Danae. She was only sixteen, which meant she couldn't give consent. I eventually could not escape the reality that it wasn't an affair; *it was rape.*

Danae moved in with my dad and eventually gave birth to two of my siblings. The abuse never stopped, but the amount of abuse my sisters Evelyn, Maggie, and I experienced was limited by the unofficial visitation agreement between my parents. Evelyn, Maggie, and I spent every other weekend at my dad and Danae's house. However, because of my mom's meth addiction, it wouldn't be long before we lived with our dad permanently.

I remember the day I heard Danae had run. My heart felt a sense of victory and happiness for her. I remember feeling like she was my hero, the bravest person I knew. I was about nine years old, living with my two younger sisters, my mom (whose meth addiction was crippling her), and her abusive boyfriend, who also had a meth addiction. I sat listening intently while the adults around me talked about how my dad had come home from work one day and found all of Danae's and my sibling's things gone. My dad had no idea where she went, who she went with, or if she and the kids would ever return.

I felt so much hope. Hope that a mother would and could protect her children. Hope that my brother and sister would live the rest of their lives free of abuse. Hope that abusers don't win, that they may have control for a short time, but they don't get to control and abuse forever. My hope was soon crushed.

My dad easily gained back control. He used Danae's drug addiction and alcoholism to legitimately prove that the kids were in an unsafe situation and needed to be found. My dad hired a private investigator to find them. He shared how he was victimized by having his children taken from him and cried when he talked about the possibility of never seeing them again. The private investigator found Danae in another state, living with a man she had been having an affair with. My dad took Danae to court and won full, I repeat *full*, custody of my siblings. My family talked about it like it was a victory. The reality was, the way my aunt lived was boundaryless and mostly unsafe; however, bringing my siblings home would not provide them safety. I remember seeing joy on my dad's face while inside feeling like he had just locked the door behind them.

I became a follower of Christ eight years later when I was seventeen. For the next ten or so years, whenever I struggled, my Christian friends, my husband and my grafted family (I'll explain later) would say things like, "God loves you", "He's with you", "He will heal you", "Just follow Him". These well-meaning messages were meant to anchor me. Instead, these messages added chaos to chaos. But God, who saw me, knew I had an anchor. He saw every detail, every wound, every survival tactic, and every fear. Therefore, He knew that my anchor would not be rooted in love, companionship, healing, or leadership. Instead, He knew my anchor was rooted in safety, and my hope would come in finding out that I have a God who is a protector.

My favorite verse in the Bible is Luke 22:31-34 (ESV), which says:

SIMON, SIMON, BEHOLD, SATAN DEMANDED TO HAVE YOU, THAT HE MIGHT SIFT YOU LIKE WHEAT, BUT I HAVE PRAYED FOR YOU THAT YOUR FAITH MAY NOT FAIL. AND WHEN YOU HAVETURNED AGAIN, STRENGTHEN YOUR BROTHERS." PETER SAID TO HIM, "LORD, I AM READY TO GO WITH YOU BOTH TO PRISON AND TO DEATH." JESUS SAID, "I TELL YOU, PETER, THE ROOSTER WILL NOT CROW THIS DAY, UNTIL YOU DENY THREE TIMES THAT YOU KNOW ME.

If this verse doesn't hold much meaning to you, please let me set the stage. Jesus, during his last Passover meal, has just explained to his followers that He will soon be crucified. He is preparing them. Jesus knew that the circumstances around His crucifixion would be devastating for those who loved Him. He knew that the crucifixion and all that led up to His death would lead to a fear so fierce within His followers that

Satan would intend to use that fear to crush them spiritually. First, his followers would watch as Jesus is betrayed by Judas, someone they all trusted. Next, they would watch as Jesus is unrightfully arrested. They would then hear and learn about Jesus being taken before Pontius Pilot, who had the authority and the power to free Jesus. Despite Pilot's power, authority and belief that Jesus was innocent, Pilot would turn a blind eye and allow Jesus to be killed. All of this resulted in Jesus being stripped naked, beaten, mocked, and tortured to death. Jesus knew that, in these circumstances, his disciples would feel fear, and amidst the fear, their hope of a savior and protector would be crushed.

In order to combat the fear and provide hope, Jesus says to Simon Peter: "Simon, Simon, behold, Satan demanded to have you, that he might sift you like wheat." Jesus tells Simon Peter that He not only sees, He foresees. He knows Satan approached God and requested to "sift (Peter) like wheat". To sift wheat, in biblical times, meant to lay the wheat on the ground and beat it with a tool that would pull the broken and withered grains away from the chaff. The chaff is a protective casing for the grains to grow safely in. Satan intended to use the circumstances around the crucifixion to pull the fear-driven believers away from Jesus. He intended to put Jesus' followers in a position where they would lose their faith, thereby eliminating them. A loss of faith would mean a loss of hope in a savior and protector. A loss of hope would separate each person from their creator, giving Satan all the power to kill, steal, and destroy.

Jesus then says, "But I have prayed for you." Jesus is saying to Peter, I know all you will see, hear, and endure will be devastating. I know it will break you, I know you will lose faith, I know you will question me, I know you will be afraid...*but but but* I won't let it overtake you. I've done the most powerful thing I can do to protect your soul—I have prayed for you.

15

Jesus protects Peter by making sure that despite Satan's efforts, Peter, although he will feel afraid and deny Christ, will not lose his faith entirely. He protects Peter by making sure the door never locks behind him. He protects him by making sure he will turn back to God to find hope, healing, and love, just as He has done for me and *you*.

Jesus then gives Peter a purpose in his suffering by saying, "When you have turned again, strengthen your brothers." In other words, Peter, when your hope in me is restored, encourage others who are in the midst of their own devastations.

Peter then says to Him, "Lord, I am ready to go with you both to prison and to death." Jesus said, "I tell you, Peter, the rooster will not crow this day, until you deny three times that you know me." Peter can't fathom being in a situation where Satan could cause so much fear that Peter would deny his belief and hope in Jesus. Peter is emphatic about being willing to follow Jesus into death. Jesus, in his empathy, shares with Peter that He knows about three fear-driven, weak moments in which Peter will compromise his beliefs and do something he will be ashamed of in order to be safe. Jesus tells Peter that He sees and He knows the compromises: "The rooster will not crow this day until you deny three times that you know me." Despite the compromises, Jesus did the most powerful and protective thing He could do for Peter–He prayed for Him.

Although my hope at nine years old had been crushed, my hope was not destroyed. We have a God who is a protector, who sees me, sees you, and sees what is *unseen*. He is a strong anchor and His unseen protection over us is something I find comfort in. If, in the midst of your abuse, you have done things you're ashamed of to keep yourself or another safe or to function when you were afraid, Jesus knows. If you struggle with belief in Jesus or your faith is weak, He knows. Before your circumstances, before your compromises, before your denial of Jesus, Jesus prayed for you so that your faith would not be destroyed. He has empathy for you. He died on a cross for you so that you're forgiven and He rose from His death to win the battle you're afraid of.

Can you hear Him saying to you, "Satan has asked to sift you as wheat, but–I have prayed for you"?

# Ponder

Consider pondering the following questions. To be gentle with yourself, I suggest pondering one set of questions a day, being as honest as possible. Have empathy for yourself in this process.

What compromises have you made to keep yourself or another safe? Do you struggle with feeling shame about these things?

When considering the compromises you made to keep yourself or another safe do you find that you beat yourself up over these compromises? Do you have a hard time forgiving yourself or having compassion for yourself? If someone you loved was in the same situation, making the same compromises would you have compassion for them?

Do you believe Jesus has prayed for you? Do you believe that His prayer for you is His powerful way of protecting your spirit? Why or why not?

Describe the circumstances where you experienced the most fear. Do you think these fear-driven moments have caused you to deny your belief in God? Why or why not?

Have you seen evidence of God's protection over you? List examples.

Have you ever considered that God has empathy, compassion, and concern for you?

# Chapter Three

## Unlearning That God

*You would not have called to me unless I had been calling to you, said the Lion.* - C.S. Lewis, *The Silver Chair*

It was late afternoon when a friend dropped me off at home after my high school softball practice. I opened the front door to find my great Uncle Ruben, who lived on the bottom floor of our two-story apartment, sitting in the dark with the TV on but the volume exceptionally low. Without making eye contact, he turned his head in my direction and silently, while making a grimaced face, shook his head back and forth, alerting me to be prepared before I made the climb upstairs. I took a deep breath while my heart sank into my stomach. I watched my feet as their heaviness landed on each step, knowing whatever was about to happen upstairs or whatever had already happened, Uncle Ruben was not going to come to our rescue, nor was he going to call for help.

With each step, I processed what my role might need to be. People talk about fight, flight, fidget, and freeze; however, the way I kept myself safe and tried to keep my siblings safe was to fawn. Fawning is a way of flattering someone or pleasing them to keep things peaceful, safe, and stable.

I knew I would need to assess what was happening at the top of the stairs and quickly make my dad feel the best about himself I possibly could. As I took the last step up, moving from the dark stairwell to the lit hallway in front of me, I looked up to see someone's blood splattered across the wall. It was silent, so I couldn't assess whose blood it was, what the circumstances were, or the location of others in the house. I put a simple, peaceful smile on my face, the kind where your mouth barely turns upward, made a right turn, and very gently in a tender voice greeted my dad in almost a question—" Hey."

He was sitting in his recliner facing the muted TV. His only response to me was, "Tell your brother to get the fuck out here and clean the blood off the walls before someone sees it." I headed straight for our bedroom where I quickly assessed my twelve year old brother for wounds that needed to be attended to while we discussed what he would need to clean his *own* blood off the walls. I gave directions to my other siblings who were in the room with us to go grab the cleaning supplies so that I could finish assessing, and to do it the best they could without being heard or noticed by my dad. My brother, with fear and anger in his voice, said, "I don't want to go back out there."

I wish I had had the power to tell him it was okay not to, but my dad had specifically said he wanted *him* to clean it up. Again, like many times before, I felt the meanness of this demand, the demeaning and cruel requirement for him to clean his own beating off the walls so that the beatings could continue to be hidden. I felt my own powerlessness and the shame from the unspoken lie that I was responsible for sending him out there. The reality was that if my brother had not been the one to do the cleaning, he would have gotten another beating, and it would have put the rest of us in danger as well. Although both he and I knew this, it was my words, my voice, and my direction telling him he had to be the one to clean his blood off the wall.

A couple of weeks after this incident, a family member told me that our Uncle Ruben had told several other family members about what was happening to us. I had an immediate moment of hope; full of relief, I took a deep breath that I hadn't taken for years. I waited. I waited for days. I waited for months. All the time thinking someone who knew would do something. No one ever did. At least not enough to make it stop, so it continued.

As you can imagine, trusting is not easy for me. I often explain it to people like this. It seems to me that people without CTD have three trust-boxes in their brain: people they trust, people they're not sure about yet, and people they don't trust. These people, once they get to know someone, can keep others in the boxes they have earned even when there are slight changes or glitches in a person's character or behavior. My brain, the way I experience it, only has two boxes: people I trust and people I don't. People move into and out of these boxes on a regular basis, despite the trust they have earned. What I mean, is that my brain takes all people, including the people I intrinsically trust, and moves them into and out of my trust and don't- trust-boxes for numerous, uncountable reasons.

For example, if my husband and I are standing in the same room and I am triggered by something completely unrelated to him, he and everyone else in that room gets moved into the "don't-trust-box" until I can process through the trigger and then do the work to move him back over to the "trust-box". I know it sounds simplistic and sad, but because I live in a state of hypervigilance, where my brain is constantly sizing people up based on safety, planning my escape route, scanning my environment, reading body language, and examining facial expressions, my trust-boxes have to be managed in seconds. More than two boxes would make having

CTD impossible to live with. Processing who is trustworthy during a trigger is a skill that has taken me years to be competent at (and honestly, I'm still pretty inconsistent). So, what does this mean for me? It means that I have to work very hard to process my relationships on a different brain pathway.

When I recognize someone that should be intrinsically trusted has moved into my don't-trust-box, I have to work hard to transfer that safe person back to the trust-box. This. Is. Exhausting.

When I first became a Christian, I also struggled to keep God in the trust-box. The poor guy got moved to the don't- trust-box probably ten times a day. This was problematic because I could not grow in my relationship with Him unless I could consider Him trustworthy. I'm not sure where I heard this, but I once heard that to have a relationship with anyone, you have to freely trust until that person proves untrustworthy. I knew that if I wanted to have a relationship with God, I had to figure out a way to keep God in the trust-box long enough to form some sort of understanding about who He is in relation to me. For me, this meant I needed to view God differently. I could not view Him as a male father-figure because I could not wrap my mind around trusting a man or a father. In my small ability to understand who and what God is, I was only able to compare him to things I knew and experiences I'd had. So sadly, God became a gross distortion of my experiences with my mom and dad, and so I hated Him.

God, who saw my hatred and had empathy for me, led me to Exodus chapter three. In Exodus chapter three, Moses is in the field taking care of a flock of sheep when he sees a bush on fire that is not being consumed. Moses becomes interested in why the bush is not burning up, so he goes over to the bush and hears God calling out his name from the bush.

Exodus chapter 3:4b-14, ESV:

"Moses, Moses!" And he said, "Here I am." Then He said, "Do not come near; take your sandals off your feet, for the place on which you are standing is holy ground." And He said, "I am the God of your father, the God of Abraham, the God of Isaac, and the God of Jacob." And Moses hid his face, for he was afraid to look at God.

Then the Lord said, "I have surely seen the affliction of my people who are in Egypt and have heard their cry because of their taskmasters. I know their sufferings, and I have come down to deliver them out of the hand of the Egyptians and to bring them up out of that land to a good and broad land, a land flowing with milk and honey, to the place of the Canaanites, the Hittites, the Amorites, the Perizzites, the Hivites, and the Jebusites.

And now, behold, the cry of the people of Israel has come to me, and I have also seen the oppression with which the Egyptians oppress them. Come, I will send you to Pharaoh that you may bring my people, the children of Israel, out of Egypt." But Moses said to God, "Who am I that I should go to Pharaoh and bring the children of Israel out of Egypt?" He (God) said, "But I will be with you, and this shall be the sign for you, that I have sent you: when you have brought the people out of Egypt, you shall serve God on this mountain."

THEN MOSES SAID TO GOD, "IF I COME TO THE PEOPLE OF ISRAEL AND SAY TO THEM, 'THE GOD OF YOUR FATHERS HAS SENT ME TO YOU,' AND THEY ASK ME, 'WHAT IS HIS NAME?' WHAT SHALL I SAY TO THEM?" GOD SAID TO MOSES, "I AM WHO I AM." AND HE SAID, "SAY THIS TO THE PEOPLE OF ISRAEL: "I AM HAS SENT ME TO YOU."

According to my husband, a Bible scholar, when Moses asks God who he should tell the Israelites is sending him, God replies, "I will be who I will be." The Hebrew can also be translated, "I am who I am." The power of this name of God is incredibly significant as it makes a profound statement opposing the boxes we often place God in based on our human, finite knowledge and experiences. I will be who I will be; I am who I am.

I have spent years unlearning and unbelieving the character of God that I made up based on my experiences. If God is my experiences, then He is manipulative, unkind, unattached, willing to destroy another to make Himself feel happier, untrustworthy, and unsafe. I'm afraid of the God I made up.

Thankfully, this is not the God of the Bible. The God of the Bible is a truth-teller, He's loving, attached, and relational, willing to sacrifice Himself for me and for you. He is faithful, good, gracious, peaceful, and a boundary-setting, safe and fierce judge. This is the God I wanted to get to know. To have a relationship with this God I had to learn His nature first. In an effort to identify and describe God's nature I've used works from Arthur W. Pink, Wayne Grudem, and Tim Keller. Although basic, the rest of this chapter is devoted to the nature of God.

**God Is Holy**

Holiness means that He is perfectly moral, completely pure, and *without*

25

evil. Arthur W. Pink says, "In scripture, He is frequently styled 'The Holy One': He is so because the sum of all moral excellency is found in Him. He is absolute purity..." God's holiness is the anchor to which I attach my trust. A God who is not evil is *safe*.

## God Is Love

Love is the nature of God, meaning it is not caused by anything. There is nothing in humans, animals, the world, the universe, or beyond that causes God to love. Love simply exists within God, which means that God loves from the source of love which is Himself. The impact of this is that His love is free. He gives love without motive, he gives love unselfishly, and He gives love regardless of our actions. God's love is always present because He is the *source* of it.

## God Is Good

Because God is holy, with no evil found in Him, perfectly moral, perfectly pure, and the source of love, *He is good*. His goodness is not determined based on our circumstances. His goodness is determined only by the definition of his nature. Out of His goodness he commands, creates, judges, sets boundaries, and rules with wisdom. Out of His goodness He wants us to have a relationship with Him.

## God Is Perfect and Unchanging

Because God is perfect He can't get any better or any worse. He is who He is whether or not we please Him. He remains the same whether or not we are obedient. He does not have good days or bad days in character. His character remains perfect despite our failures and the ways we hurt each other. He remains faithful and He keeps his promises. Wayne Grudem says, "...our faith and hope and knowledge all ultimately depend on a *person* (God) who is infinitely worthy of trust-because he is absolutely and eternally unchanging in his being, perfections, purposes, and promises."

## God Is All-Powerful

God's power, because He is without evil, the source of love, good and unchanging in character and nature, is used to produce things that are good. For example, from His power He casts out demons, sets boundaries, calms raging seas, creates beauty, heals the sick, and forgives sin. Tim Keller, in his book, the *Reason for God*, says, "At first sight, then, a relationship with God (who is all-powerful) seems dehumanizing. Surely it will have to be "one way," God's way. God, the divine being, has all the power. I must adjust to God- There is no way that God could adjust to and serve me. ...it is not true in Christianity. In the most radical way, God has adjusted to us-in his incarnation and atonement. In Jesus Christ, he became a limited human being, vulnerable to suffering and death. On the cross he submitted to our condition-as sinners-and died in our place to forgive us." We only benefit from an all-powerful God who is the source of love.

## God Is Eternal

When there was nothing, there was God. When there was no Earth, no angels, no galaxy, no universe, God existed. He existed before anything else and will exist when other things come to an end. Therefore, His love is eternal with no beginning and no end. His holiness is eternal, meaning he will never stop being holy. His goodness has no beginning and will have no end. His reign has no beginning and no end, He will be unchanging forever and his power will never be weakened or strengthened because His power is unchanging having no beginning and no end.

## God Is Spirit

God is not male or female. He is not restricted by place, time, or space. He can be in all places at one time, dwell in humans, and be felt by humans without being seen by them. Because I can't say it any better than Wayne Grudem in his book, *Systematic Theology*, I will simply quote him. "God does not have a physical body, nor is he made of any kind of matter like much of the rest of creation. Furthermore, God is not merely energy or thought or some other element of creation. He is also not like vapor or steam or air or space, all of which are created things: God's being is not like any of these. God's being is not even exactly like our own spirits, for these are created things that apparently are able to exist only in one place in one time." Because God is Spirit He can be with us always. There is nothing more comforting than a good and loving God with no evil as part of His nature, always with us.

## God Is All-Knowing

God is all-knowing, even able to know our thoughts. "You have searched me, Lord, and you know me. You know when I sit and when I rise; you perceive my thoughts from afar. You discern my going out and my lying down; you are familiar with all my ways. Before a word is on my tongue you, Lord, know it completely." (Psalm 139:1-4, NIV)

God, who sees you, knows all that you think of Him. He knows all the ways you have distorted who He is because of your experiences. He is gracious and compassionate and will give love despite your distorted beliefs of Him. If you find that trusting God is difficult because you have created a God in your mind that looks like your abuser, unlearn *that* God. Your abuser's actions are not God's actions, your abuser's thoughts are not God's thoughts and your abuser's words are not God's words. The God who says, "I will be who I will be, I am who I am," doesn't look anything like your abuser. Instead, He loves you and He wants a safe and good relationship with you.

# Ponder

Consider pondering the following questions. To be gentle with yourself, I suggest pondering one set of questions a day, being as honest as possible. Have empathy for yourself in this process.

List the characteristics about God you believed (and may still believe) before reading about the nature of God. How have your thoughts and beliefs about God changed since reading about the nature of God?

Sit for a moment and process what perfectly moral, completely pure, *without evil* means in regard to someone you can trust. Would you feel safe in this relationship?

How does it feel and what does it mean for you to hear that God loves you independent of your thoughts, behavior, or faithfulness? How does it feel and what does it mean for you to learn that you're loved because God is the source of love? Does learning this change your perspective on God loving the parts of you that feel unlovable?

I used to hear Christians saying, "God is good" and it made me angry. However, now that I understand that they were referring to God's nature being good and not my circumstances, I share the same perspective. What is it like to read about God's nature being good?

As a newer Christian, a perfect and unchanging God was such a difficult concept for me to process. I was used to drastic emotions in my intimate relationships, emotions that determined if I would be screamed at or beat up. A God that is unchanging feels safe to me. Can you trust an unchanging God?

I used to believe that having an all-powerful God meant that I could be punished in the most horrendous ways. Knowing a God who uses His power for good is a concept I often have to meditate on. Do you want to know and trust this God? What did an all-powerful God mean to you before hearing about His goodness? What does it mean to you now?

# Chapter Four

## Do I Believe You?

*The world outside has not become less real because the prisoner cannot see it.* - Tolkien, *On Fairy-Stories*

I can't remember why dad was angry. I don't remember who was lying on the floor beneath him, who ran to the door, and who was screaming, "Get help." I have such a disassociated memory of the incident that I can't tell you. I know it happened. I asked one of my sisters if she remembered this particular beating, and she said she thought it was me on the floor, but I can't remember lying there.

What I do remember is that the beating taking place was so terrifying that for the first time, one of us yelled to the other to get help. I remember my dad's words clearly, "If you open that door, I'll put her in the hospital." I won't ever forget the feeling of defeat as my sibling took a step away from the door and my body went limp as the beating stopped.

*We believed him.*

What my dad said about hurting us was believable because he hurt us. We watched it and we experienced it, and so it was believable. My dad's actions made it easy to believe what he said.

I attended a Bible college for my undergraduate degree and had to write a paper in one of my classes on the attributes of God. I received a C on that paper, and I wasn't happy because I thought I had turned in a solid A paper. After class, I approached the professor to ask why I was given a C. He told me it was because I was missing several important, loving attributes of God. I told him that I didn't include those attributes because I didn't believe them to be true. I remember his empathy when he asked if he could pray with me and his continued empathy after, annoyed, I told him "No," but that he was welcome to pray for me on his own.

I was angry that I was being held accountable for something I didn't understand and couldn't comprehend. That C left me feeling frustrated with the obvious disconnect between what I was learning about God's goodness, love, and holiness and what I actually experienced in the nineteen years leading up to that moment. However, God, who knew I lacked experience in being loved, also knew that believing Him would be difficult for me. So He guided me to His Word that is filled with pages and pages of metaphor to describe what His goodness, His love, and a relationship with Him *could* look like. Although I will forever have a C on that paper, God was faithful in building a way for me to bridge the disconnect between the *truth* I was learning about Him and what I had experienced.

The Bible uses many, varied metaphors to describe the attributes of God because we cannot fully describe God using one metaphor. These metaphors are there to help us grasp important concepts about God and to give us a way to connect with Him.

One particular metaphor that significantly impacted my

understanding of God's love for me is God as a mother. God is described in the Bible as being like a mother in labor, a nursing mother, a mother who comforts, a mother who has compassion on her child, a mother with keen attention to her child, and a mother bear who will protect her cub. Although my own mother, who struggled with meth addiction and housed an abusive boyfriend, facilitated an environment that perpetuated neglect and abuse, I was able to relate to this passage because God allowed me to be a mother myself and, in doing so, taught me about Himself.

I can still remember nursing my daughter. I remember her latched, her eyes staring at my face while she ate. She was building a reliance on me that would intrinsically define her trust in me. She was learning to trust that I would meet her needs, bring her comfort, and find joy in her that would grow an attachment and connection of love between us. Once weaned, this trust must have been seared on her heart because, over the years, she would continue coming to me, believing I would provide for her, believing my love was lasting, and believing in my tenderness.

In Psalm 131:2-3 (ESV), King David talks about his relationship with the Lord in this way: "But I have calmed and quieted my soul, like a weaned child with its mother; like a weaned child is my soul within me. O Israel, hope in the Lord from this time forth and forever more." After breastfeeding and weaning my own child, I could understand the depth that King David must have trusted and believed God, the deep hope he must have had in the Lord, and the deep connection between them.

The metaphor of God being like a mother anchored my belief in God's goodness to something I had experienced. As my belief started to grow, I was able to believe other Bible passages that previously were difficult to fathom. For example, when I read Psalm 86:15, ESV, "But you, oh Lord, are a God merciful and gracious, slow to anger and abounding in steadfast love and faithfulness," I could grasp that this could be true about God's relationship with me. I would picture myself with my baby girl and allow these words to penetrate my heart and believe that if I could feel this way about my daughter, God could feel this way about me.

It's one thing to *know* about God; it's an entirely different thing to have a *relationship* with Him. A relationship with a good and loving God, whom you believe, transforms loneliness, hope, fear, and insecurity. The power of this kind of relationship in my life transformed my shame into gratefulness, my loneliness into comfort, my need to survive into a need for attachment and connection, and my fear, a fear that owned me, into something I could use for good.

If you feel the disconnect between what you're learning about God and what you believe about Him because you lack experience being loved, cared for, or treated with value, tell Him. Starting your relationship with God in a place of honesty is the best place to start. He loves you and He wants a relationship with you. He can help you reconcile the disconnect through metaphors He shares about Himself, new experiences, and new relationships.

Are there any metaphors in the Bible describing God that you can trust and relate to? Here are a few to think about: God as a potter, who takes a purposeless, lifeless slab of clay and finesses it into something beautiful, made useful, giving it a purpose. "But now, oh lord, you are our father; we are the clay, and you are our potter; we are all the work of your hand." (Isaiah 64:8, ESV)

God is described as a shepherd, one who provides for and protects those under his care. "The Lord is my shepherd; I shall not want. He makes me lie down in green pastures. He leads me beside still waters. He restores my soul." (Psalm 23:1-2, ESV) Another metaphor is Jesus (God) as a vine who gives nourishment and life to its branches (believers): "I am the vine; you are the branches. Whoever abides in me and I in him, he it is that bears much fruit, for apart from me you can do nothing." (John 15:5, ESV)

The metaphor I struggled to relate to for years was God as a father. My dad, never having taken ownership of his behavior, having emotions that swung to extremes multiple times in a day, who hurt us and had mean and demeaning demands, kept me, for a long time, from being able to connect with any male figure in an authoritative position over me. The idea that I could have a relationship with God that was not a dictatorship was a foreign concept. When the Bible uses words like "submit", which, in context, is one of the most loving words used regarding relationships with each other, I was unable to imagine anything other than "Put yourself in a degrading or vulnerable position."

So, there was a season in my life when I allowed myself to rest in God's attributes that felt safe and decided that getting to know God in those ways was good enough. In that season, I was relieved to not have to get to know God as a father. However, as my relationship with God grew, I became more aware that I was lacking something because of not knowing His fatherly attributes. The truth is, God is in the business of redeeming and restoring and *He wanted to restore my understanding of a father*. To not know God as a father would keep me from knowing God fully and from healing some deep wounds. God knew I would suffer from only knowing Him in part and not continuing to grow in my understanding and relationship with Him.

In my slow process of trusting God, I was able to use metaphors that were not masculine to believe in God's good attributes. This allowed me to build a foundational relationship with Him so I could bridge and reconcile those attributes with the masculine ones.

God, knowing that I would struggle to believe that there would be no evil in Him as a father, also provided, over the years, a husband who is kind and whose relationship with our daughter I learn from. He provided a dad, through my grafted family, that helped bridge the gap for me by being safe and showing lovingkindness. Slowly I began to believe what God was saying about Himself as a Dad who wants a relationship with me.

If you struggle to trust God's masculine attributes, you may not believe it yet, but God is a good Dad who wants a relationship with you. He wants to share with you the fullness of who He is. He wants healing and restoration for you.

# Ponder

Consider pondering the following questions. To be gentle with yourself, I suggest pondering one set of questions a day, being as honest as possible. Have empathy for yourself in this process.

Are there any metaphors in the Bible or any metaphors mentioned in this chapter, describing God, that are difficult to trust, believe or relate to?

Do you believe that your past experiences are not what God wanted for you? Why or why not?

Your belief about God's character will define your relationship with Him. Are you afraid of Him? Do you spend all your time obeying rules and being obedient in order to not be punished? Do you believe you need to perform well, act or look a certain way to be loved by God? Do you have a tender relationship with Him where you spend your time being comforted, asking for help, and seeing Him as a loving Father and Friend? The answer to these questions should give you insight into what you believe about God.

Are you ready to know God's fatherly attributes? Is there another attribute of God that is directly affected by your story? Are you ready to know this part of God yet?

Write a list or description of a good God's attributes. You may need to go back to chapter three and reread about God's love and goodness before writing your list or description.

How is the above list or description different from what you've experienced in your life?

# Chapter Five

## He is My Boundary-Setter

*Scripture is full of admonitions to separate ourselves from people who act in destructive ways. We are not being unloving. Separating ourselves protects love because we are taking a stand against things that destroy love.* - Henry Cloud and John Townsend, *Boundaries*

**The following memories are meant to depict the chaos of trust in an abusive home.**

My eyes flashed open. I was lying in bed next to my sister who was already awake. His voice screaming "girls" drove us to start kicking each other as we fought over who was going to get up and respond to him. My sister made the argument that she went last time and, out of fear that our negotiation was taking too long and could result in a beating, I threw the blankets off and rushed to the living room. He sat in his recliner watching TV. "Make me a sandwich," he said. I hurried to the kitchen, made him his sandwich, gave it to him, and turned to hurry down the hall back to my bedroom before he could ask for a kiss goodnight. I was never quick enough and, even if I had created distance between us, his yell reached the end of every room in the apartment. "Aren't you going to give me a kiss goodnight?" In that moment, despite the fear, I knew it was best for all of us, to show him affection. I kissed him on the cheek and hurried back to bed.

His face said that he was proud that I had played a good game and so I felt special.

As I woke up, I took a second to process what I was hearing. I took a deep breath in as relief came over me. The loud music and his voice singing over it meant that he would be dancing in the living room. It meant, in that moment, there would be peace.

My dad, angry about something, looked me directly in the eyes before calling me a fucking cunt. For the first time, realized that to survive the next couple of years before graduation, my purpose would be to absorb his anger.

It was so cold in the house. My mom woke us and guided my sisters and me to the gas heater in the living room. We stood in front of the heater while we put on the clothes she had laid out. She put my hair in a ponytail, helped us get our jackets on, and walked with us to the bus stop. I felt loved.

My brother opened the front door to find his mom (my aunt) standing there. She said a quick hello to the five of us kids then held out a small wad of cash toward my dad. "It's in the bedroom," he said while motioning with his head in the direction of the bedroom and turning to walk down the hall. She tried to avoid following him, "No, just bring it out here." He denied her request by saying, "Naw, com'on, put your money away I have to talk with you about something." She always followed. I didn't have to be told that he required a sexual favor for the drugs – they were always in there just long enough for me to know nothing could have been talked about. I could see the disappointment on her face as she followed him and wondered in that moment if she would feel fear while showing affection.

I couldn't watch it any longer – the beating taking place – so I stepped between them. He paused, set down the plastic, hard-shelled, CD case he was about to chuck at my sister, and charged at me. "You think you can save him?" With his push, I landed on the floor and immediately put my shins up like a shield to protect the rest of my body from his repeated kicks. I followed his kicks with my shins and just before he bent over to hit me I saw in his eyes that he was missing. His awareness, his logic, his humanness was missing amidst his rage. In that moment I was more scared than I ever remember feeling.

We were playing at the park while my dad played in his soccer game. I was hungry. I asked for the keys to the truck because I knew he kept snacks under the driver's seat. I unlocked the truck door, grabbed the snacks from under the driver's seat, and ate, feeling taken care of.

We told my mom he was hurting us but when she confronted him, he told her we were saying the same thing about her ...she believed him. She kept sending us to stay with him until she decided we should live there permanently.

Trusting people feels chaotic when you believe they have the freedom to treat you however they like based on how they're feeling about themselves, about you, or about their circumstances. Growing up there were no distinct lines drawn between a person I loved and cared for, and a person who was supposed to love and care for me, and what kind of treatment I should expect from them. The result, as an adult, was to fear all relationships, trusting no one.

The sad thing about me not trusting people is that I assumed everyone lived this way. So, I didn't understand how my husband and I could attend the same event where the activities at the event were intended to foster relationships and he could say, "That was so much fun, let's hang out with them again," and I could say, "You think they like us? Why would they like us? How could you tell they liked us?" I would then list all the possible negative intentions they had with wanting to hang out with us again. The dichotomy between my husband's trust and my lack of trust in people was so extreme I would conclude that he was a fool and, therefore, a liability, someone whose opinion I shouldn't trust. All of my relationships felt exhausting, chaotic, and unsafe.

The harsh reality is that not having anyone to trust means not having anyone to attach to, so I felt lonely all the time. This is problematic because humans were not created to be alone. God intended for us to love each other and to rely on each other, for our relationships to be used for companionship, safety, and connection. God created humans to need one another and to be attached to each other, *but not without boundaries.*

Living my life not trusting anyone only made my life more difficult, lonelier, and more chaotic. However, I didn't have a road map for how to attach to someone and I couldn't seem to let my guard down long enough to figure out how to do it on my own. I was feeling hopeless and stuck when I heard of a program at our church called Mending the Soul. I signed up for the grueling, twelve-week group therapy program that was designed to help adult men and women, who had been abused, find healing. I liken this program to getting shot with an arrow and then having someone slowly pull it out. I say this with gratefulness and a little bit of a side-wink. It's necessary; the removal of the arrow is required for living a healthy life. However, the painful process of removing it is something I never want to do again. That said, I would encourage anyone I love, who has suffered abuse, to participate in this program.

Although the Mending the Soul book and workbook for men and women did not give me a road map for attachment, it did lay out the characteristics of an abuser. As I read through the list, I felt a sense of safety I had never felt. Having a defined list of characteristics to look out for in other humans gave me, for the first time, a set of guidelines to navigate which people in my life might be trustworthy and which ones might not. This new set of relational guidelines gave me a sliver of what is called *felt safety*. Once I knew what *felt safety* felt like, I wanted more.

According to *The Connected Child*, Felt safety is a strategy used to help others feel safe through changes in behavior and changes in the environment. In my case, this list of characteristics, although informational, gave me a sense of safety and control. I liken it to fishing off the side of a boat in the open ocean. While in the boat you can fish with ease, knowing you won't drown, and sharks won't eat you. It allows you to sit back, enjoy the sunshine and find pleasure in your activity. However, if the boat was taken away you would be boundaryless. You would be floating in open water trying to keep afloat and hoping no sharks are around. You wouldn't enjoy the activity at all. Instead, you would probably stop fishing altogether and constantly search the water for predators and do your darndest to find the shore or a rock to perch on.

Being handed a list of abuser characteristics was like being handed two oars while drowning in the ocean and realizing that, where there are oars, there is probably a boat.

At the end of the twelve weeks, the facilitator of our class offered to lead me and a friend through a book called *Boundaries* by Dr. Henry Cloud and Dr. John Townsend, which took my desire for felt safety to the next level. I was realizing that I had absolutely no boundaries. I had, for thirty-something years, been floating in open water. There were no lines drawn in my life to help me determine where I ended and where someone else began. Until that point, I had an underlying belief that I was only worth how other people treated me. Sometimes I was used to absorb someone else's anger; sometimes I was used to share in someone else's joy. But I never considered that my value and purpose could be determined by myself and by God.

This new idea – that I could decide what I liked and didn't like, what kind of behaviors I was going to produce, and what kind of behaviors I was willing to tolerate – brought an exciting hope I hadn't felt before. I wish you could see my *Boundaries* workbook – it's marked up everywhere with "wows" and exclamation marks. Every idea seemed new, especially the idea that I could say "yes", and I could say "no" based on what I wanted and what God considers good. I think it's important that I emphasize that my boundaries were created with God's guidelines in mind, primarily because God's parameters are the *ultimate* good. And, honestly, because my home as a child was void of good examples for boundaries, scripture provided a place to start.

I will talk about attachment in future chapters. However, one necessity for trusting someone enough to attach to them, at least for me, was having boundaries. Without boundaries, I do not feel safe enough to attach. Dr. Becky Kennedy, in her book, *Good Inside*, gives a clear explanation of boundaries as she addresses parental boundaries with children. "Boundaries are not what we tell kids *not* to do, boundaries are what we tell kids we *will* do."

Boundaries are part of the continuing list of God's nature I spoke about in chapter three. In *Boundaries*, Cloud and Townsend state,

THE CONCEPT OF BOUNDARIES COMES FROM THE VERY NATURE OF GOD. GOD DEFINES HIMSELF AS A DISTINCT, SEPARATE BEING, AND HE IS RESPONSIBLE FOR HIMSELF. HE DEFINES AND TAKES RESPONSIBILITY FOR HIS PERSONALITY BY TELLING US WHAT HE THINKS, FEELS, PLANS, ALLOWS, WILL NOT ALLOW, LIKES, AND DISLIKES. HE ALSO DEFINES HIMSELF AS SEPARATE FROM HIS CREATION AND FROM US. HE DIFFERENTIATES HIMSELF FROM OTHERS. HE TELLS US WHO HE IS AND WHO HE IS NOT. FOR EXAMPLE, HE SAYS THAT HE IS LOVE AND THAT HE IS NOT DARKNESS. (I JOHN 4:16; 1:6, NIV).

God is self-aware and has self-control, which allows Him to limit what behaviors He allows and lets His "yes" mean "yes" and his "no" mean "no" without control or resentment of others. He sets clear parameters and tells the *truth* about who He is. Because boundaries are part of God's nature, boundaries are written and set in place all over the Bible.

Isaiah 42: 8 NLT says, "I am the LORD; that is my name! I will not give my glory to anyone else, nor share my praise with carved idols." God is saying here that He does not want us to worship other gods or idols because He alone deserves glory and He will not share that glory. Flowing from His knowledge about Himself, He knows what He is, and is not, willing to tolerate.

God states what He *will* do if we worship other Gods. Exodus 20:4-6 (NIV) states,

YOU SHALL NOT MAKE FOR YOURSELF AN IMAGE IN THE FORM OF ANYTHING IN HEAVEN ABOVE OR ON THE EARTH BENEATH OR IN THE WATERS BELOW. YOU SHALL NOT BOW DOWN TO THEM OR WORSHIP THEM; FOR I, THE LORD YOUR GOD, AM A JEALOUS GOD, PUNISHING THE CHILDREN FOR THE SIN OF THE PARENTS TO THE THIRD AND FOURTH GENERATION OF THOSE WHO HATE ME, BUT SHOWING LOVE TO A THOUSAND GENERATIONS OF THOSE WHO LOVE ME AND KEEP MY COMMANDMENTS.

I will talk about image-bearing in a future chapter, but God in his boundary setting also has our best in mind. Paul Copan, in his book, *Is God a Moral Monster?* Says this, "Humans are 'imaging' beings, designed to reflect the likeness and glory of their creator. If we worship the creaturely rather than the creator, we'll come to resemble or image the idols of our own devising and that in which we place our security."

God allows us to hate Him but not without consequence. He allows us to hear His boundaries and not respect them, but not without consequence. He tells us He will let us live in our own ways without Him, resulting in generations of a family not knowing, understanding, or experiencing God's love. The consequence is being separated from God. The natural consequences of living a godless life will eventually make us long for God and come back to Him. This is one example from God's list of boundaries.

I have set similar relationship boundaries. For example, I will not tolerate being hit by my spouse. If hitting becomes a part of our marriage, I'll divorce him.

I started looking into this idea of boundaries as a set of parameters to help define myself – what I'm okay with, what I'm not okay with, and what I'm willing to do in response to someone else's behavior.

Coming up with a list of things that defined me meant that I had to acknowledge my current list: The person to absorb others' anger. Expendable. Unloved. Disgusting. Not worth enough to be treated with kindness, dignity, or respect. This list meant that in the wake of someone else's behavior, I would cower, keep quiet, carry shame, and live without a sense of self.

If this list changed, how would I be defined? For example, if my list read: loved, important, worthy, intelligent, strong, and brave then my boundaries would sound like this: you're allowed to talk with me this way; if not, I will...you're allowed to touch me this way; if not, I will... you're allowed to speak about me this way; if not, I will...

Trusting people becomes easier when you, with God's good in mind, get to define who you are and set limits, consequences, and boundaries on what others can and can't do to you.

Throughout the book of Proverbs, you will find what I call "boundary wisdom." Before I married my husband, I was afraid because I didn't know what red flags to look for to know whether or not I was making a good decision in choosing someone with good character. While living with a friend's family, that I would eventually be grafted into, the dad in that family directed me to Proverbs and told me to read through them and highlight phrases and descriptions that sounded like my boyfriend (at the time). He told me to pay attention to how many phrases were highlighted that addressed a foolish person versus a wise person. This direction was instrumental in my saying "yes," with confidence, to my husband's proposal. Below are a few examples of the wisdom God gives in Proverbs about people's character that can easily give direction on where to start when creating your boundaries:

**"As a dog returns to its vomit, so fools repeat their folly"** (Proverbs 26:11, NIV). If a person in your life repeats the same foolish behavior what consequences or boundaries will you set?

**"Make no friendship with a man given to anger, nor go with a wrathful man"** (Proverbs 22:24, ESV). Do you care for someone who is angry and wrathful? If so, is this the kind of relationship that aligns with your and God's definition of yourself and how you should be treated?

**"A man of great wrath will pay the penalty, for if you deliver him, you will only have to do it again"** (Proverbs 19:19, ESV). How many times are you willing to let a wrathful person off the hook? How many times are you okay with keeping this person from their consequences? Every time you allow the wrath without consequence or boundary you should expect the wrath again.

**"Wine is a mocker, strong drink a brawler, and whoever is led astray by it is not wise"** (Proverbs 20:1, ESV). Are you okay and comfortable with someone who is "led astray" in unhealthy ways by alcohol? Is this the kind of life you want? If not, what will your boundary be?

**"Precious treasure and oil are in a wise man's dwelling, but a foolish man devours it"** (Proverbs 21:20 ESV). Do you care for someone who understands the treasure they have, do they care for it, save it, value it, and cultivate it? Or, does this person you care for squander their treasure, burn through their earnings or undervalue it? Which one are you, the wise or the foolish man? Which one is your loved one, the wise or the foolish man?

Trust is chaotic if you're swimming in open water. I hope this chapter is the equivalent of handing you two oars. Where there are oars, there is a boat. God did not consider it good for you to live in chaos; He is a boundary-setter who wants you in loving and trusting relationships with others.

# Ponder

Consider pondering the following questions. To be gentle with yourself, I suggest pondering one set of questions a day, being as honest as possible. Have empathy for yourself in this process.

Does trusting people feel chaotic to you? Why or why not?

Do you have boundaries and parameters that define you? If so, list them.

Do you find yourself making statements like "all men are unsafe," "all women are unsafe," "all police officers are unsafe," "all black people are unsafe," "all white people are unsafe," "all pastors are unsafe," or "all churches are unsafe"? Have you considered that these extreme statements come from a boundaryless place? That you might feel safer when it comes to an entire people group if you learn how to set boundaries and learn that you can have control and power in healthy ways rather than aggressive, untrusting, or hateful ways?

Do you find yourself worried about how someone will treat you if you set a boundary?

Have you ever had someone reject you or call you a name because you set a boundary?

What defines you? Where does your identity lie? How you define yourself and your identity determines what you're willing and not willing to allow in your life. Write out a description of your current identity (use the next activity to help you with this).

# Activity

Below is a statement of basic truths I used years ago to define myself. Reflect on these statements. From these statements begin to write down what defines you.

I am a child of God, an image-bearer. I am a believer in Jesus, forgiven. I live in the presence of the Holy Spirit, I am an heir to the kingdom of Heaven, meant to be in the full presence of God. I will never be abandoned. I belong, as a member of the body of Christ. My spirit is protected by Jesus' sacrifice for me, His death has made me eternally right with God. I was created to be in loving relationships, maintain boundaries, create, and care for the things God cares for. I am dearly loved. God delights in me, and my presence is enjoyed. The Lord God rejoices over me with gladness, He will quiet me with His love. I am God's workmanship, His handiwork, He restores my soul and is the savior of my story.

# Chapter Six

## Why Did You Allow It?

*Why, then, did God give them free will? Because free will, though it makes evil possible, is also the only thing that makes possible any love or goodness or joy worth having.* - C.S. Lewis, *The Case For Christianity*

The phone rang. I was alone in my dorm room when I picked it up. "Hello?" My brother, who had relied on me our whole lives to help manage my dad's anger and advise him on how to get through one of his rages with the least amount of harm possible, was on the other end of my hello.

"Evangeline? It's Kevin."

"Hi? What's going on?" I asked.

"I ran away from home and I'm scared."

"Okay, where are you?"

"I'm at Danielle's house. Her mom said I could stay here as long as I need. I'm safe right now but Danielle's mom doesn't know how bad it is. Dad called and acted all nice and asked Danielle's mom if he could talk to me to work things out. When I got on the phone he told me that if he ever ran into me in town, he would tie me to the back of his truck and drag me down the street until I was unrecognizable."

He believed our dad and he wanted my help to know what to do next. I told him to lay low and I tried to comfort him by telling him that this would blow over and that I would call our dad and try to smooth things over. I hung up the phone and immediately dialed my dad's number.

My dad picked up right away. I told him I was just calling to say "Hi." He shared that my brother had run away and that he was angry about it. I remember, fawning, making my brother sound like a flippant, irresponsible teenager whose hormones were raging and who, of course, wouldn't want to live somewhere else. I referred to memories of my dad at that age and asked him if he remembers making dumb decisions and encouraged him to call my brother up and ask him to come home in a couple of days.

Managing my siblings' safety from afar was never something I planned to do and I realize now that I never truly helped anyone. However, over the years, the numerous times the police and foster system were called never helped either. Once I left for college, I made it a goal to never live at home again. The summer between my freshman and sophomore years of college I worked as a maid in a hotel. The hotel was located on a Christian campground and part of the compensation was my room and board. I was beyond grateful for this opportunity and, of course, relieved to not have to spend the summer at home. However, the next summer I couldn't find a place to work where I could also live. I was becoming increasingly anxious about what I was going to do so I shared my anxiety with some friends (providing only limited details).

One of my friends, Ruth, responded to my anxiousness by asking her parents, Michael and Ella, if I could come home with her for the summer. They agreed and found me a job. Ruth's dad, Michael, is a farmer-turned-pastor who once worked at a boys' ranch. Her mom, Ella, is a farmer's wife- turned-pastors wife who holds a lot of strong opinions and doesn't waver easily. They have a lot of grit and stamina for long-suffering when it comes to encouraging others' relationship with Jesus. Very quickly it was easy for me to determine that, at least for the summer, they would be safe.

During the first few weeks I was there, I watched how Michael treated his wife and children. As I waited for the "shoe to drop" and his anger and rage released, I grew increasingly envious of the way his children were treated and began asking the question, "Why me?"

One afternoon I followed Michael to the backyard. I was so hurt to watch his kids treated in kind ways by him and Ella that my questioning about why God allowed me to be abused began to surface. "*Why me? Why did He allow it?*"

I yelled my questions at Michael about why God allows suffering. He put one hand in his pocket and talked with the other, "Well, that's a tough one, Evangeline. I can tell you right now that I know God loves you and that He didn't want you to suffer. And I can tell you that if you ask Him that question He'll be faithful to answer it and bring you comfort while you work it all out. I'm guessing I'm not quite sure all of what you're asking in that question, but it may help you to start by thinking about *free will* and to see what the Bible says about it." Then he told me where to start reading.

Ugh, I wanted to avoid writing this chapter because, just like Michael answering that question for me, I don't know what kind of anger you carry. I don't know what exactly lies behind the question and I don't know the contempt you hold against God. It's taken years for me to hash out the details of this question with Jesus and there are moments and seasons even today that I still get angry about free will. So, to think I could answer this question in a chapter seems ridiculous. The most honest thing I can do is tell you what Michael told me and then do my best to give you a starting point in the Bible.

So you, who have known the craziest kind of suffering, I can tell you right now that God loves you and that he didn't want you to suffer. If you ask Him why He allows suffering He'll be faithful to answer you and bring you comfort while you work it out together. I'm guessing I'm not quite sure all of what you're asking in your question, but the problem is not that He allows suffering but that he allows free will. Suffering is simply a consequence of free will. When I'm angry at God, it's not because of suffering. It's usually because God created man in his own image, giving man free will. My accusation is usually, "What were you thinking?"

Genesis 1:26-31a (NIV),

Then God said, "Let us make mankind in our image, in our likeness, so that they may rule over the fish in the sea and the birds in the sky, over the livestock and all the wild animals, and over all the creatures that move along the ground."

So God created mankind in his own image, in the image of God, he created them; male and female, He created them .God blessed them and said to them, "Be fruitful and increase in number; fill the earth and subdue it. Rule over the fish in the sea and the birds in the sky and over every living creature that moves on the ground." Then God said, "I give you every seed-bearing plant on the face of the whole earth and every tree that has fruit with seed in it. They will be yours for food. And to all the beasts of the

EARTH AND ALL THE BIRDS IN THE SKY AND ALL THE CREATURES
THAT MOVE ALONG THE GROUND— EVERYTHING THAT HAS THE
BREATH OF LIFE IN IT—I GIVE EVERY GREEN PLANT FOR FOOD." AND
IT WAS SO.

GOD SAW ALL THAT HE HAD MADE, AND IT WAS VERY GOOD.

The two italicized words in this passage above are "subdue" (*kavash* in
Hebrew, Strong's number 3533) and "rule" (*radah* in Hebrew, Strong's
number 7287). Since humans are created in God's image, these verbs,
in context, imply taking care of God's creation in a kind, respectful and
generous way, similar to how God interacts with the world He created.
Plants and animals are provided to sustain mankind and mankind is to
lovingly care for plants and animals in an interdependent relationship.
Even more important, humans are to relate to each other in kind, respectful, generous, and just ways. This way of relating to creation in the
right way is what the Bible calls *shalom*. *Shalom* (Strong's number 7965)
is a Hebrew word that is often translated "peace" or "welfare" but it has
a much deeper, rich meaning.

In *Not the Way It's Supposed to Be*, Cornelius Plantinga, Jr. explains
*shalom* as follows:

THE WEBBING TOGETHER OF GOD, HUMANS, AND ALL CREATION
IN JUSTICE, FULFILLMENT, AND DELIGHT IS WHAT THE HEBREW
PROPHETS CALL SHALOM. WE CALL IT PEACE, BUT IT MEANS FAR
MORE THAN MERE PEACE OF MIND OR A CEASE-FIRE BETWEEN EN-
EMIES. IN THE BIBLE, SHALOM MEANS UNIVERSAL FLOURISHING,
WHOLENESS, AND DELIGHT – A RICH STATE OF AFFAIRS IN WHICH
NATURAL NEEDS ARE SATISFIED AND NATURAL GIFTS FRUITFULLY
EMPLOYED, A STATE OF AFFAIRS THAT INSPIRES JOYFUL WONDER

AS ITS CREATOR AND SAVIOR OPENS DOORS AND WELCOMES THE CREATURES IN WHOM HE DELIGHTS. SHALOM, IN OTHER WORDS, IS THE WAY THINGS OUGHT TO BE.

God, giving us dominion and the responsibility to subdue what He created, is asking that we cultivate and rule in a way that uses the earth's resources and human creativity to do good for others, to take care of each other, and to love each other. In this responsibility, humans are distinct from everything else He created. There is intelligence and empathy in this responsibility, the ability to have compassion and understanding about other species and to learn from them by observing them. To subdue and have dominion in this context, gives us the responsibility to take care of creation and other species by being in relationship with them. It means we have been given the ability to choose and given a sense of what is just. Justness requires a standard. People's independent standards only result in chaos. A supernatural standard is from God.

The beauty of being an image-bearer is that it was intended to be lived out within a relationship with God, and intended to give us the freedom to restore, to heal, to love, and to change. Image-bearing extends to us the responsibility to take good care of ourselves, our relationships, and the environment around us. Being an image-bearer allows us to make good moral decisions based on the ability to discern the difference between good and evil, right and wrong. "Right" being God's definition of what is good and evil and "wrong" being to reject what God considers good and evil.

Let me be clear, He did not make us gods. He made us image-bearers giving us great responsibility but setting boundaries to protect us from the knowledge of evil. God's intention for us to be fully human was meant for us to live only in goodness. He created Adam and Eve to live amongst the tree of the knowledge of good and evil but told them *NOT* to partake in it. I wonder if Adam and Eve who spoke with the serpent and trusted him, lived with the serpent, as they did all the other animals; taking care of him, having compassion on him, finding beauty in him, and building a relationship with him while maintaining an intimate relationship with God, trusting God's goodness, and respecting God's protective boundary over them. Adam and Eve did not know evil until they used their free will to decide good and evil for themselves.

NOW THE SERPENT WAS MORE CRAFTY THAN ANY OTHER BEAST OF THE FIELD THAT THE LORD GOD HAD MADE. HE SAID TO THE WOMAN, "DID GOD ACTUALLY SAY, 'YOU SHALL NOT EAT OF ANY TREE IN THE GARDEN'?" AND THE WOMAN SAID TO THE SERPENT, "WE MAY EAT OF THE FRUIT OF THE TREES IN THE GARDEN, BUT GOD SAID, 'YOU SHALL NOT EAT OF THE FRUIT OF THE TREE THAT IS IN THE MIDDLE OF THE GARDEN, NEITHER SHALL YOU TOUCH IT, LEST YOU DIE.'" BUT THE SERPENT SAID TO THE WOMAN, "YOU WILL NOT SURELY DIE. FOR GOD KNOWS THAT WHEN YOU EAT OF IT YOUR EYES WILL BE OPENED, AND YOU WILL BE LIKE GOD, KNOW-ING GOOD AND EVIL." SO WHEN THE WOMAN SAW THAT THE TREE WAS GOOD FOR FOOD, AND THAT IT WAS A DELIGHT TO THE EYES, AND THAT THE TREE WAS TO BE DESIRED TO MAKE ONE WISE, SHE TOOK OF ITS FRUIT AND ATE, AND SHE ALSO GAVE SOME TO HER HUSBAND WHO WAS WITH HER, AND HE ATE. THEN THE EYES OF BOTH WERE OPENED, AND THEY KNEW THAT THEY WERE NAKED. AND THEY SEWED FIG LEAVES TOGETHER AND MADE THEMSELVES LOINCLOTHS. (GENESIS 3:1–7, ESV)

Adam and Eve lived within God's intended boundaries for His im-age-bearers, choosing from their own free will to believe and obey that what God considers good is actually good. This changed when they decided that what the serpent was saying about God might be true. Maybe God was lying to them. The serpent was clever in manipulating the idea of death as God's lie and was good at convincing Eve that what God considers good might actually be Him withholding something from them.

Out of Adam and Eve's freedom they chose good for themselves, believing that knowing evil wouldn't cause death. However, humans continuously err on the side of selfishness, control, cowardice, a lack of self-control, and hate. These choices then lead to corruption, shame, and abuse, which directly oppose God's intended purpose for image-bearing humanity. God was telling the truth, choosing good and evil for ourselves leads to a spiritual death, separating humans from their relationship with God and requiring a physical death as payment for sin.

We are given the right by God to make choices that have drastic effects on ourselves and others, both for good and for evil. God always gave us the choice to know evil; He let Adam and Eve know the tree existed. However, he asked them to choose to not partake in it. He asked them to *choose his way*.The difference between God and us is that there is no evil in Him. Therefore, when and what He chooses is always good. The cowardly choice is not an option for Him; the selfish choice is not even a consideration. However, it is for us. We are not bound by God to only make the good decision; He gives us the freedom to choose or reject what He considers good and what He considers evil.

It's become a habit for me over this past year to call my kids image-bearers. I use this name both as an affectionate reminder and an acknowledgment of the beauty they hold when they have done something kind and loving or when their presence simply brings joy. I have also used this name as a cuss word when I recognize, through their free will, they have used their image-bearing privilege for selfish reasons. The struggle is present in all of us so identifying my children as image-bearers often helps me give my children more grace and it reminds me of the ways I've taken advantage of my own free will. It breaks my heart to watch my children make poor choices that hurt themselves and others. This sadness is also part of image-bearing.

An example of sadness being an image-bearing trait is found in the story of Noah and the flood. Only six chapters into the Bible, God becomes grieved as He watches humans live out so much selfishness and evil,

THE LORD SAW THAT THE WICKEDNESS OF MAN WAS GREAT IN THE EARTH, AND THAT EVERY INTENTION OF THE THOUGHTS OF HIS HEART WAS ONLY EVIL CONTINUALLY. AND THE LORD REGRETTED THAT HE HAD MADE MAN ON THE EARTH, AND IT GRIEVED HIM TO HIS HEART. SO THE LORD SAID, "I WILL BLOT OUT MAN WHOM I HAVE CREATED FROM THE FACE OF THE LAND, MAN, AND ANIMALS AND CREEPING THINGS AND BIRDS OF THE HEAVENS, FOR I AM SOR-RY THAT I HAVE MADE THEM." (GENESIS 6:5-7, ESV)

Tim Mackie says,

(THE FLOOD) IS A SOBERING PORTRAIT OF GOD'S JUSTICE. GOD IS NEVER SAID ONCE TO BE ANGRY IN THAT STORY. WHAT THE INTRO-DUCTION SAYS IN CHAPTER 6 IS THIS: THE LORD WAS SORRY THAT HE MADE HUMANS ON THE LAND AND HE WAS PAINED, HE FELT PAINED IN HIS HEART. GOD'S JUDGMENT IS TO RELAX HIS ORDERING POWER AND TO GIVE HUMANS OVER TO WHERE THEY CAME FROM AND WHERE THEY'RE GOING TO, WHICH IS BACK TO THE DUST AND IT'S TO REMOVE HIS ORDERING POWER FROM THE COSMOS AND AL-LOW CREATION TO COLLAPSE IN ON ITSELF AGAIN. THE WAY THAT

GOD JUDGES IS TO HAND PEOPLE OVER TO THE OUTCOME OF THEIR DECISIONS.

Being an image-bearer means continued grieving over evil and suffering in the world. Grieving for us and grieving with God. Sometimes I'm still mad at God for making us image-bearers because the nature of image-bearing is human choice, it's free will. I sometimes wish God would have commanded humans to follow him without option, to not think or choose or decide for ourselves.

Although God confines evil choices to work and result in His ordained good for His people, although He has a redemption plan, a way to deal with and manage the damage that results from human choice, He still grieves and continues to grieve over your abuse. He didn't want you to be abused. He didn't allow it and watch with pleasure. My dad abused me, yes, but before he abused me, he rejected what God considers good and what God considers evil. My dad defined good and evil for himself. God was already grieved before my dad ever laid a hand on me because the moment he rejected God's good, God knew there would be damage to everybody around him.

# Ponder

Consider pondering the following questions. To be gentle with yourself, I suggest pondering one set of questions a day, being as honest as possible. Have empathy for yourself in this process.

Have you ever considered that God was grieved that He made humans? How does it make you feel knowing that your suffering grieves Him?

God created you as an image-bearer, communicating the beauty and glory and goodness of Himself through you. When you hear that you're an image-bearer, how does that impact you?

Do you currently (or have you in the past) struggle with the belief that God thought you deserved the abuse, even earned it somehow?

Are you angry at God for your suffering? If so, what do you accuse him of...not stopping the abuse? Allowing the abuse? Allowing free will?

After reading this chapter do you believe God, did not want you to be abused?

Do you believe that your abuse was a result of your abuser defining good and evil for themselves? In other words, do you believe that if your abuser had defined good and evil according to God's definition you would not have been abused?

Are you able to recognize that if you're angry at God, most likely you *do* believe in Him?

# Chapter Seven

## Is Your Justice Good News?

*Justice at its best is love correcting everything that stands against love.* - Martin Luther King Jr., *The Autobiography of Martin Luther King, Jr.*

The summer going into my sophomore year of college my dad beat my sister up, finally sending one of us to the hospital. Amongst other things, my sister had multiple wounds to her face and head; wounds terrible enough for my dad to be arrested and tried in a court of law.

If you don't know much about child abuse cases, depending on the state you live in, in order to be convicted of a felony, the abuse needs to be potentially life-threatening or have the potential to cause health problems.

My dad was convicted of a felony and served weekends in jail and weekdays on house arrest for a year (with the exception of going to work). He was required to take a certain amount of child abuse and anger management classes before *welcoming* my brothers and sisters back into the house. My dad plead guilty to willful harm – injuring a child and endangering health. I was never sure why he plead guilty unless it helped reduce his punishment. He spent years explaining to people that he barely hit my sister and that she was exaggerating.

I helplessly surrendered to the fact that he got away with dehumanizing my sister, first by beating her to satisfy his anger and second by minimizing what he had done instead of taking ownership. It left her to think she was crazy rather than validate the awfulness of what he had done to her.

Over the years, every beating he got away with made him more comfortable with his behavior. He was so comfortable that a beating horrific enough to cause the wounds my sister suffered wasn't noteworthy enough to hide.

To the woman who saw the beating and was brave enough to follow them home and call the police, thank you.

The justice system, by considering this beating a first-time offense, in my opinion, did not punish to the degree that was deserved. The injustice of my dad's punishment only perpetuated and reinforced my CTD. When the system did not provide what I believed to be actual justice and I had to watch my dad's offenses minimized and mercy shown to him, the fear I always lived with settled deeper in my being. Where would I ever go to feel and be safe? Who would ever protect me, if, despite the evidence, my dad's punishment was so minimal? Even today, in my mid-forties, I am still afraid of my dad. Maybe I'm afraid of him because every bone and nerve in my body was trained to be afraid. Maybe I'm afraid because I watched him for over twenty years get away with abuse and minimize what would affect me for the rest of my life without true consequence.

The judge had no authority to determine justice except what humans authorize as good. And apparently, to humans, weekends in jail and house arrest during the week for a year, with the exception of going to work, was considered good justice. The irony that guilt gets to be determined by someone who doesn't have to live with the wounds is hysterically maddening, like a person going crazy in a padded room type of maddening. The reality is, despite it being the first time my dad was caught, it was by far not the first time he abused. My dad's sins and the ramifications of those sins are first against God and then against those he abused. God hates what my dad did. The judge that sat in that courtroom made his determination on the physical evidence of *one* offense. He did not see all that God saw and he did not grieve in the ways God grieved. He did not and will not live with the ramifications of my dad's destructive behavior on mine or my siblings' mental health, and he did not and won't have the responsibility to heal my wounds or my siblings' wounds.

As much as I have talked about God's goodness and love, I haven't addressed the fact that His perfect, pure, and holy nature requires obedience. It requires obeying and honoring all things God considers good. God, being without evil does not mean God is without justice. Throughout the Bible, alongside the other good and loving descriptions of God, God is also described as the God of justice, the God of vengeance, and the God who is jealous and wrathful. These characteristics of God made me fearful at first, the kind of fear that made me not want a relationship with Him before I *understood* his goodness. Once I understood his goodness, however, I could trust him as a good judge.

In our humanity, which is filled with evil... vengeance, jealousy, and wrath are not good. However, vengeance, jealousy, and wrath existing *without* evil is a beautiful kind of justice.

Although God is tolerant in that He allows the existence of opinions or behavior that He doesn't agree with, He is *not* boundaryless. When the goodness of God is abused and humans make the decision to define good and evil for themselves this is called sin. God is very clear that He hates sin and that the payment for sin is death. Even in Genesis, when God tells Adam and Eve not to eat from the tree of the knowledge of good and evil, he says, "You will surely die." What he meant is that the knowledge of evil would result in sin and the consequence of sin is death.

So what does the payment of death for sin look like? It looks like hell. Hell, as described in the Bible, is a place where God does not dwell. It is the absence of God, a fiery eternal torment, filled with gloomy dungeons and worms that eat the decaying bodies that live there. A place where there is weeping and gnashing of teeth, where the condemned will have their hands and feet tied when thrown in.

Now, I'm not going to lie, picturing hell does bring me some satisfaction. The idea that maybe my dad, with his hands and feet tied, could be teetering on a plank over the fiery depths of hell and I could walk over with a bounce in my step and a whistle in my heart, stick one little finger out and push him in... feels. so. satisfying.

However, even the pleasure I find in the thought of pushing my dad into a torturous forever opposes the goodness and love of God. Therefore, I am sinning. God, although he hates wickedness, finds no pleasure in sending his creation to suffer (Ezekiel 33:11). My pleasure is *my* definition of good. And so, even in my pleasure, I am defining good and evil for myself. Also, this idea that I would get to be the one to push my dad in reveals my own desire to be the judge, determining my dad's eternity; this is also sin.

I'm comforted knowing that I don't need to be the judge because I have a good judge who hates good and evil when defined by humans. Even the good, humans muster up, is not good enough. It's what the Bible calls "defiled," which means spoiled. The absolute best that humans can offer is still wrought with selfishness, cowardice, and deception. If God didn't care about the difference between right and wrong, good and evil, then there would be no consequence for my dad or me.

I would live in a boundaryless world where my abuser gets to decide, without consequence, what is right and what is wrong...and so would I. The beauty of God and the safety I find in Him is that He is the determiner of right and wrong. God having a standard is why justice and the desire for it exist in the hearts of humans. I rest in the fact that I want justice because I am an image-bearer, but what do I do with the fact that I am also a sinner? I hope in what the Bible calls *good news*.

The good news Christians talk about is that, as image-bearers, we hold an unimaginable value and are deeply loved by God, created to be in an eternal relationship with Him. God's love for us is so profound that the Bible says even angels are astonished by God's relationship with us (1 Peter 1:12.) God, wanting an eternal relationship with us, but knowing the debt for our sin is death, decided to take our place, dying on a cross to provide a death that would pay off all our sin debts. *This is good news!*

Jesus, who is God, became human, was born of a virgin named Mary, lived as a human, restraining much of his true power and glory, died on the cross to pay the debt for our sin(s). God, in His love for us, without compromising His boundaries, provided an opportunity for us to spend eternity with Him by sacrificing Himself on our behalf.

God provided the only sacrifice legitimate enough to pay off our debt - Himself. The plan all along was for Jesus to be the sacrifice humans needed to pay the debt for their sin(s). Jesus' death on the cross served as the payment for my sin and I couldn't be more grateful.

The beauty in Jesus' blood being the ransom for my sin is that I get to take as long as I need to process, heal, forgive, and work out my issues. With Jesus as my sacrifice, I am in a good relationship with God as I do all these things. And, because I accept and believe that Jesus' sacrifice is the only thing that restores my relationship with God, God gives another undeserved gift to help me work out my issues – the Holy Spirit.

I go through cycles of forgiveness for my dad. I find that I forgive him and then when the next layer of hurt surfaces, I need to forgive him all over again. In each step of my process, the Holy Spirit is with me to heal, guide and restore. On a side note: forgiving doesn't mean I don't have boundaries. Because my dad has never taken ownership or apologized for what he's done, he has no place in my life. My mom, on the other hand, takes ownership of the hurt and destruction she's caused as she recognizes it. Therefore, I have a relationship with her, and just like any other relationship I have, I maintain my boundaries with her.

I have gratitude for Jesus and the *good news*, however, I have also had to address the reality that all of this doesn't sound like good news when I think about the possibility of my dad becoming a believer in Jesus and not being punished for his sin. Two truths give me peace and keep me trusting in God as a good judge. First: God sees what is unseen by me in my dad's life and childhood. He is aware and knows much more than I do about my dad's past and present. I don't know who the author of the quote is that says, "Hurt people, hurt people," but I do believe this is true. Second: the Bible says that there is a judgment day. Judgment day is the time when all of us will be in the full presence of God and be accountable for our choices that follow our definitions of good and evil. Although I'm not sure what this will look like, or even when it will be, I can imagine, based on what scripture tells us about the holiness of God, it won't be filled with joy and peace. If hell is being fully and completely separated from God for eternity, being fully and completely surrounded by evil then, being in the full presence of God on judgment day will be the complete absence of evil and the complete presence of our most powerful, holy, and glorious God. When I picture this I can only fathom fear, a feeling of being the smallest speck of dust in the universe. I imagine thinking, *Oh, shit!* I will have to account for the choices I've made that have come from my definitions of good and evil and so will my abuser.

Let me paint a picture for you about the full presence of God as described in the Bible. Even with the description below, the full presence of God is inconceivable.

God says to Job,

"WHERE WERE YOU WHEN I LAID THE EARTH'S FOUNDATION? TELL ME, IF YOU UNDERSTAND. WHO MARKED OFF ITS DIMENSIONS? SURELY YOU KNOW! WHO STRETCHED A MEASURING LINE ACROSS IT? ON WHAT WERE ITS FOOTINGS SET, OR WHO LAID ITS COR-NERSTONE—WHILE THE MORNING STARS SANG TOGETHER AND ALL THE ANGELS SHOUTED FOR JOY? WHO SHUT UP THE SEA BEHIND DOORS WHEN IT BURST FORTH FROM THE WOMB, WHEN I MADE THE CLOUDS IT'S GARMENT AND WRAPPED IT IN THICK DARKNESS WHEN I FIXED LIMITS FOR IT AND SET ITS DOORS AND BARS IN PLACE", WHEN I SAID, 'THIS FAR YOU MAY COME AND NO FARTHER; HERE IS WHERE YOUR PROUD WAVES HALT'? HAVE YOU EVER GIVEN ORDERS TO THE MORNING, OR SHOWN THE DAWN ITS PLACE, THAT IT MIGHT TAKE THE EARTH BY THE EDGES AND SHAKE THE WICKED OUT OF IT?" (JOB 38:4-13, NIV)

"I am the Alpha and the Omega," says the Lord God, "Who is, and who was, and who is to come, the Almighty." (Revelation 1:8, ESV)

In the complete presence of God, angels cry out to one another, "Holy, Holy, Holy is the Lord God Almighty; the whole earth is full of his glory." (Isaiah 6:3b, NIV)

"By the word of the Lord, the heavens were made their starry host by the breath of his mouth." (Psalm 33:6, NIV)

"And whenever the unclean spirits saw him, they fell down before him and cried out, "You are the Son of God." (Mark 3:11, ESV)

"Each of the four living creatures had six wings and was covered with eyes all around, even under its wings. Day and night they never stop saying: 'Holy, holy, holy is the Lord God Almighty, who was, and is, and is to come.'" (Revelation 4:8, NIV)

"(God) who alone is immortal and who lives in unapproachable light, whom no one has seen or can see. To him be honor and might forever. Amen." (1 Timothy 6:16, NIV)

Habakkak 3 explains how the monumental task of shifting the earth, scattering the hills, and turning over the mountains is a display of the Lord doing a task that *hides* his power.

Knowing that this description of God's presence is limited by human words, I have to consider that the full presence of God on Judgment day will be so overwhelming that I and my abuser will be wrought with distress. I meditate often on recognizing that, because of my human limitations, I often make God small. The idea that my dad will have to stand before this God brings me comfort that allows me to surrender my desire to be the judge and find joy in trusting that God is a good and ultimate judge. I find hope in it for the justice I want.

As inspired by Matt Heard: God longs to be with us in heaven. He does not want us to spend eternity in Hell; rather He wants our image-bearing beauty restored.

Although I will not see justice while on this earth, I live comforted that God has boundaries and limits and things he will not put up with without consequence. I rest knowing that my dad will be accountable for the beatings, the anger, the lies, and the rage on judgment day. Handing over justice to be dealt with by God allows me to focus on healing, forgiving, and growing. God's justice is good news. Jesus' sacrifice on the cross paid my ransom. He asks me to believe that His death is worth enough to make the full and good payment for *my* sin. And, I believe.

If you believe you're an image-bearer and you also believe that Jesus' death is enough for you to be completely right with God, then you're not only an image-bearer, but also a friend of Jesus, an heir to the kingdom of God, adopted as a child of God, a member of the body of Christ and the recipient of the precious gift of the Holy Spirit. If you still carry anger or recognize new layers of anger as you heal, wanting to decide justice yourself, God knows. He doesn't want you to carry it, to hold the anger so tightly that you can't heal or forgive. So, consider giving your version of justice to God and let Him be the good judge.

# Ponder

Consider pondering the following questions. To be gentle with yourself, I suggest pondering one set of questions a day, being as honest as possible. Have empathy for yourself in this process.

Have you forgiven your abuser? Do you find that, as you heal one layer of hurt another is surfaced and more forgiveness is needed?

What does justice look like when you address it from your definition of good and evil? Do you think this kind of justice is what God considers good? Why or why not?

Do you believe Jesus' death on the cross is enough to forgive your sin? Why or why not?

Had you ever considered what the full presence of God would look like or feel like? How do you think your abuser will respond to the full presence of God?

# Chapter Eight

## Trading My Shame for Grace

*Fear produces the obedience of slaves; love engenders the obedience of sons* - J. W. Sanders, Jr.

### Sounds Like Post Traumatic Stress Disorder

My dad was angry because my youngest sister, a pre-teen, had made a smart remark under her breath. We stood on the other side of the dining room table dodging the knives he pulled out of a wooden knife block to throw at us. I can't remember if the open hand beating on my back was immediately following or if it was a completely different incident. I don't remember it hurting, but the raised purple and reddish-blue, hand-shaped bruise was something I had to keep hidden when I went to school. Today, when I see a knife block, I get a sick and sad feeling, typically a flashback and sometimes a feeling of distrust towards the owner. Then I have to work through it.

## Sounds Like Paranoia

The man walking down the sidewalk bordering my suburban house did not belong there. I didn't recognize him as living in my neighborhood. I originally caught a glimpse of him out of our second-floor window while our three-year-old daughter played in the loft. I watched him walk down the street until he was out of sight. Then I walked downstairs and stepped out my front door to make sure he kept walking. Once he was out of sight from that angle of our property, I locked the doors and started planning multiple escape routes out of our house depending on where he might enter; just in case he was there to hurt us.

## Sounds Like Depression

I was so tired and sometimes so sad that I would just lay there. I wanted to get up because I had things to do and things I was interested in, but my physical exhaustion kept me there even though I had already slept ten hours. I lived like this for years.

## Sounds Like Obsessive Compulsive Disorder

I was exhausted and I wanted to go to bed. Both my children were asleep and my husband was working. I had locked all the doors an hour earlier *and* had checked them two times. I laid down in bed and closed my eyes but knew I couldn't fall asleep unless the doors were checked again.

## Sounds Like Postpartum Depression

My daughter was a couple of months old and sleeping in her crib next to our bed. My husband was lying next to me sound asleep. I got up and unlocked every door and window in the house hoping that someone would break in and take my baby's life. I felt such horrible sadness that I had brought an innocent child into a world where she would suffer. I hoped the burden of suffering would be taken from her.

## Sounds Like Attachment Disorder

At any given moment I felt I could pack my things and leave. I believed I wouldn't feel joy or sadness about leaving my husband or daughter.

## Sounds Like Anxiety

My husband asked me to go to a concert with him. I love music and I love concerts but I didn't want to go because of the crowds. I wouldn't know anyone but him and, feeling like I needed to dress up, I worried I'd be noticed and maybe even considered pretty, which would require me to be even more on guard than I already felt I had to be. I was worried about where we would find a parking space and what time of night we would leave the concert and how many drinks my husband would have even though we have a two-drink limit that he typically respects.

These and many other stories like them led my husband and myself to see multiple therapists over the years. None of which helped us make much progress other than the occasional tools to help us communicate typical marital problems in healthier ways. Over the years, it has been suggested by therapists and doctors that I have had one or more of the above disorders or mental illnesses. These professionals suggested either medication or environmental changes that never helped. Eventually, my husband and I started seeing a counselor who, after hearing the stories and asking many questions, sent our marriage into chaos when she told my husband and me that she thought I should be diagnosed with paranoia and put on medication for it. She then told my husband that he should be concerned about our daughter's safety. After just a few sessions, this woman's analysis of me dismantled our twelve-year marriage. *My husband believed* I had paranoia and *I believed I didn't.* The trust I struggled to maintain between us was completely broken and fear replaced it. My husband became afraid of my coping mechanisms because he was afraid I might hurt our daughter in order to keep her from suffering or hurt her by making a mistake when trying to manage a perceived fear. I spent one night in a hotel and, during that night, realized the importance of getting a diagnosis that actually fit me. I figured the alternative to this would be sitting in divorce court listening to someone share my coping mechanisms, without context, leaving me with the possibility of a court system deeming me an unfit mother. Within a few weeks, I began seeing a psychologist who specialized in trauma.

At the age of thirty-four, I sat in my psychologist's office quietly processing as she explained my diagnosis: Complex Trauma Disorder. It was heartbreaking. I thought, "You mean after all the beatings and the name calling and the meanness, instead of getting a gold fucking metal, you're telling me I have a mental illness?" And then, almost immediately, I began dealing with shame.

For me, my diagnosis meant that I didn't have everything under control. Shame. I had failed at managing myself. Shame. I was failing my daughter because I couldn't white- knuckle myself into coping well. Shame. I needed help. Shame. In every stage of the grief process, anger, denial, bargaining, depression, and acceptance, shame accompanied me.

It was shame telling me I would never gain credibility with anyone if they knew I had a mental illness. It was shame

saying, "You're so needy, you're exhausting for people to

be around." It was shame's voice I heard saying, "You're so weak, your daughter would be better off without you." The sneaky thing about shame is that sometimes you don't know you're carrying it until it isn't there anymore. Shame, when given power, has the ability to lead your choices, navigating you into dark and isolating places. Shame has the ability to keep you from engaging with others and asking for help. I wasn't sure how to shake it, so it settled within me and held me burdened like a heavy, but comfortable blanket.

A few years ago my husband and I started fostering with the intention to adopt. I, of course, thought that we wouldn't qualify to foster or adopt because I had CTD. The shame was consistent in reminding me of my lack of credibility. However, the caseworker doing our home study felt differently. She suggested that I might be a great foster parent because I could relate to the kids placed in our home who have experienced trauma, specifically trauma by a primary caregiver. We were eventually certified and our first placement was a sibling set of three. I fell in love with these three kiddos right away. I felt a deep connection with the younger and struggled through a rough first month with the older two. The struggle gave way to mutual respect and a trust that was easy. By the end of that first month, we were told that these three kiddos would be up for adoption. We were asked if we would be willing to adopt them and excitedly, and sadly for them, knowing this meant a great, unfathomable loss and deep grief, we said "yes."

The court hearing addressing parental rights was scheduled to happen the next month so we felt it was important to start discussing this with the kids and helping them to understand that we wanted them and had said yes to adopting them. We intended to settle their fears about being moved again since they had already been moved two times before coming to our home. It wasn't long after this that the caseworker disclosed that one biological parent had been, in the past, a safety concern in the previous homes. Although we knew this, the case worker went into further explanation regarding the concerns and gave us other pieces of information that triggered something deep within me. She needed to know if we felt we could keep the kids safe.

Over the next week, I found myself moving back into old patterns. I was startled easily and got angry at every little thing. While my husband was at work I was staying awake all night, peering out my blinds in a dark room when cars would drive by. I called the police on a car I didn't recognize that was parked in front of our house. Side note: to the high schoolers who were in said car, sorry, not sorry, that your car was towed, all your alcohol confiscated, and that your parents had to pick you up.

I knew the answer to the caseworker's question - "No." No, I don't think I am capable of keeping the kids safe from this type of possible threat. No, I don't think I can stay healthy, and no, if this threat became a reality I would not be able to protect myself let alone all four children. I felt anger, betrayal, sick to my stomach, sadness, and shame.

I felt beyond horrible telling the kids they would have to move again. Shame. That we weren't going to adopt them, shame. That, yes, we were another set of adults that made promises we weren't going to keep. Shame. Shame that that sweet boy that I love, who I still pray for, gave me one last hug and asked if we were going to adopt a different little boy. Shame. Shame. Shame. So. Much. Shame.

Several weeks after the kids moved, I was stopped at church by our pastor. He asked how I was doing in regards to this situation and I told him I was struggling. His response to me was, "God's Grace is sufficient for you and it's also sufficient for them."

"...and it's also sufficient for them."

There it was. After years of settling into shame, not knowing how to rid myself of it, I was handed the lightest, warmest, most beautiful comforter I had ever put on. A gift to replace the burdensome blanket of shame: *grace*.

As a new believer in Jesus, the definition of grace had a significant impact on my life once I understood the meaning of mercy. Mercy, in general, means that the one who has the ability to punish for wrongdoing will have leniency or forgiveness toward the one at fault. Therefore, instead of getting a maximum sentence, the one at fault would be given half that sentence or, instead of taking the full punishment, the one at fault would be pardoned. Mercy is a pardon of some or all of the fault. Mercy sounds good until you hear about grace. Grace is mercy on steroids.

Grace takes mercy to the next level by first forgiving our fault and then by providing an added undeserved gift. J.I. Packer said it beautifully in his book, *Knowing God*: "Grace means God's love in action towards people who merited the opposite of love."

In 2 Corinthians 12:9b (NIV), Paul reports Jesus saying to him, "My grace is sufficient for you, for my power is made perfect in weakness." Paul tells the Corinthian church to boast about their failures because, in their boasting about what they have broken and what they can't do, they will get to say, *BUT* God. They will get to give the glory to God for redeeming the broken, shameful things in their lives.

Amidst our trauma, we often hurt others, but there is hope. I can't wait to one day hear from the children who lived in our home. My hope is, despite my failures, they will say, "Although you caused us more trauma, God in his loving grace protected us; God healed our hurts; God comforted us; God gave us a home and a family; God redeemed it all!"

The truth is, I can say this about God in my own life. Despite the abuse from my dad, despite the addiction and neglect of my mom, I can say, *BUT* God! God allowed my brain to do the smartest, most intelligent thing for survival. He provided me with loving relationships. He led me to get a diagnosis. God was doing the healing and redeeming of what they made broken and He is *still* redeeming it all.

Based on God's good, holy, and loving character, *shame does not come from Him. Shame is not something God gives, it's something God redeems.* Shame is not meant to be carried. God, acting in love, and having compassion on us, keeps us from being blanketed by shame by offering his loving grace. Forgiveness plus an undeserved gift-a restored relationship with God.

# Ponder

Consider pondering the following questions. To be gentle with yourself, I suggest pondering one set of questions a day, being as honest as possible. Have empathy for yourself in this process.

Is shame keeping you blanketed up and comfortable? So disturbingly comfortable that you won't ask for help? What kind of help do you need?

Does shame accompany you because there was a confusing pleasure in your abuse or conflicting messages of love in the midst of neglect or another form of abuse?

Can you replace your shame with the truth and the acknowledgment that God's grace is sufficient and you're not meant to be the hero of your story? God is.

Do you believe that God will take care of and fix the things broken in you? Do you believe that God will take care of and fix the things you broke?

In coping with your childhood abuse or in your managing of CTD, have you made choices that have led you to carry shame? What are they?

Have you hurt another person in the process of coping? Do you carry shame because of the hurt you caused? If so, do you believe God will intercede to care for them? Do you believe His grace is sufficient for them?

If you need help, list the people or places you could turn to to ask for or get the help you need. Write names, addresses, and phone numbers.

# Chapter Nine

## He Uses It for Good

*With the goodness of God to desire our highest welfare, the wisdom of God to plan it, and the power of God to achieve it, what do we lack? -* A.W. Tozer

I was playing outside, in the sun, with my sister. It was the kind of playing I see in my own children; the kind in which they are so lost in the moment that they live in abandon, losing all sense of what is happening around them. So much so that they ignore their thirst and their need to pee. The kind of playing that propels them to burst into the house to get another toy they need to prolong their joyful play.

I remember being about seven and filled with this same kind of abandon and joy. I needed something from inside the house so I ran through the backdoor which opened to the kitchen. Our kitchen was small, the usable walking area was approximately five feet by five feet. Adjacent to the back door was the only non-occupied wall in the kitchen. My mom was sitting upright on the floor with her back against the wall and her left arm above her head in a protective position. Her head was tilted down toward the floor, but as I burst through the door her eyes immediately lifted to meet mine. Her boyfriend, at the time, was standing over her in a way that I knew he had put her there. With a forced, high-pitched voice, that was supposed to sound like joy, and a smile on her face, my mom said, "Evangeline! Go outside and play, we'll be out in a minute." Her boyfriend just stood there. He didn't look at me, He didn't say anything, he didn't lock any doors behind me, but that old familiar feeling came back and, as I looked at my mother, who couldn't protect herself, I knew she wouldn't be able to protect me either.

The pervasive relational nature of the different forms of long-term abuse that I experienced stole my abandon. Over the years, though I wasn't aware, to fill abandon's gaping absence would be some of the most tactical, hypervigilant, survival skills my little brain and body could muster. I would eventually carry these skills into adulthood, unaware that I was using them. Throughout my daily interactions, I would be triggered by something and cope with that trigger by having paranoid behaviors. Hours later I would experience another trigger that I would cope with using OCD-type behaviors. Later I might cope with a trigger by using fawning behaviors; still, later I might take a second shower and a nap, sleep for hours and then sleep my regular eight hours that night to cope with another trigger, looking like I was depressed. These behaviors, though they looked like the main problem, were actually behaviors used to manage triggers when my body was in fight, flight, freeze, fidget, or fawn. Sometimes these behaviors were healthy responses to triggers or perceived threats and sometimes they were unhealthy.

I had to acknowledge that CTD once served me; however, it now *owned* me. I needed to transform it into something that served me again. My goal became to manage my CTD in healthy ways. My psychologist asked if I wanted to manage it with medication or exposure therapy. She explained, at the time, that there was no medication specifically designed for CTD so I would have to consider depression and/or anti-anxiety medication. Since I had already tried medication for depression and didn't want anti-anxiety medication, I opted for exposure therapy.

Because my husband is an adventurer, for years I found myself in situations where I was unknowingly using exposure therapy by teaching myself healthy ways to cope with triggering environments. For example, when my husband and I would snorkel and I felt scared, I would practice slower, more controlled breathing techniques. When we backpacked through Italy and my husband asked an old woman if she knew of anybody who had a bedroom we could sleep in (because he thought it would be nice to take a break from sleeping in a tent), I forced myself to perseverate on things that were generally good about humans and how my husband loved me and would choose to protect me if something happened to me in a stranger's home. When we lived overseas and traveled to unknown areas or surrounding countries, we had to make decisions on which route to take based on lighting, political tension, crowds, etc. I didn't know it then, but I was already practicing what CTD had naturally trained me to do.

So, through a series of questions, my psychologist gathered a list of all the strategies I was already using to manage triggers in my environment. Then she gave us homework and met with us once a week. Over a four-to-six-week period, we were tasked with three things: working together, identifying triggers, and shifting perspectives. My husband took a month-long sabbatical from his job and we spent each day focused on these three tasks.

**Task one:**

My psychologist pointed out that one major problem was that I was managing my CTD alone, which puts all the pressure for safety on me. It keeps me isolated and from living in healthy abandon. In order to determine if my husband was onboard, willing to work on our marriage and willing to trust me, I had to help him understand my perspective through a CTD lens. With the help of my psychologist, I explained how I see the world while living with CTD.

I explained that home owners, insurance companies, and the fire department worry about houses burning down. Their worry is not due to paranoia, but due to their own experience or knowing someone it has happened to. Therefore, these people and organizations see a house fire as a real threat and, in order to address the threat in a healthy way, they encourage others to keep fire extinguishers around the house, plan escape routes, decide on a meeting place, and place fire detectors in each room of the house. Unhealthy ways of dealing with this type of real threat might be telling families they can't ever cook in the house or require that an electrician check the wiring in the house every Monday morning to avoid a fire. Healthy or unhealthy, *all* of these actions are taken to manage a threat. Just in case you're wondering, unhealthy is defined as something that is impeding your daily life/function. Having a fire extinguisher on-hand would not impede my living but not being able to cook a meal in my house would.

My husband began listening to the perspective that my childhood was much more traumatic and much more violent than his. Therefore, my current behaviors don't mean I'm paranoid; instead, they are actions taken because my brain, for survival, prepares itself for what it knows.

Therefore, it is reasonable to be aware of real threats and that there are clear and reasonable expectations for managing these threats in *healthy* ways. My husband had to begin to acknowledge that, in the same way a fire department prepares for a possible fire, the healthiest thing for me was to prepare for a possible attack or assault. He also had to get to the point of understanding that my brain developed to survive and protect me from the people in my life that were the closest to me and who were supposed to care about me. So, if I couldn't trust the people closest to me, I wasn't going to be able to trust the world, especially people that aren't supposed to care about me.

Once my husband was onboard, I had to acknowledge that I was never including my husband in any of the considerations and processes that dominated my thoughts. I needed to start including my husband in my safety plan. The remarkable thing was that once I started including him, he was able to see that my perceived threats were valid and reasonable. I was almost immediately able to let a sliver of my guard down knowing that I wasn't alone and that someone else could help manage a situation if necessary.

For example, during my husband's sabbatical, we took our daughter to a Disney movie at the movie theater. After selecting a strategic spot in the theater to sit, I explained to my husband the strategy behind this particular seating arrangement and how it allowed me to scan my environment and get to an exit quickly. Prior to this conversation, my husband simply thought my selection of the seat was my preference for how I liked to see the movie screen. While my daughter and husband chatted away before the movie, I sat quietly scanning the environment and eventually noticed a man in his forties walk into the theater. He had a large belly, he was alone and was wearing a trench coat. I was immediately concerned because he was middle-aged and in a children's movie with no children. He was wearing a coat that could easily conceal a weapon and he was overweight which could indicate depression. My cortisol levels were raging and my signals for danger were going off like crazy. I shared this with my husband. He reassured me that it was probably nothing and suggested the guy may be one of those adults who likes to wear Disney ears at Disneyland. But he didn't stop there. He asked if it would help me if he walked down and hung out for a little bit around the guy to check him out and make sure he didn't have a weapon when he took off his coat. I agreed and when my husband came back indicating the man did not seem to have a weapon on him, was sitting with snacks, and seemed to be interested in the movie, I was able to let my guard down a little while keeping one eye on the movie and one eye on the guy.

For the first time, my husband was able to understand how intense that activity must have felt for me and how he and my daughter could walk out of the theater having had a great time and connecting and how I could walk out having had a stressful time and was just glad *we survived*. By involving my husband in my process, I had a partner, I was no longer alone. Not only did this take some of the stress off, but my husband was able to see the reality that I was not experiencing the same connection, attachment, or joy that he and my daughter were.

The other shocking realization about including my husband in understanding my triggers, hypervigilance, and tactical strategies was I became aware of how much I was doing all day long without even recognizing it. It helped to give me a clear picture of the amount of energy I was putting into managing my day.

**Task two:**

Throughout my day I needed to identify triggers. Most triggers were easy to identify because I would physically startle or feel immediate anger. For example, if I was sitting in the passenger seat of a car and we hit a speed bump too fast, while others might laugh, I would become angry almost to the point of having an inner rage and hatred for the driver. If someone dropped something creating a loud crashing sound, I would become angry. If we were at the playground and I watched a little boy fall and scrape his knee, my startle would dramatically exceed the normal reaction of the boy's mother.

Another indication that I had been triggered was my distrust of someone close to me, again usually accompanied by anger, but without an obvious reason. The first Sunday I started processing my triggers, we decided to visit a church near our home. Within seconds of walking into this church, I felt a distrust toward my husband; an anger toward him like he was my enemy. Per the direction of my psychologist, I immediately pulled my husband aside and told him that I felt that I couldn't rely on him, that I didn't trust him, and that I was angry at him. He asked what I thought caused it. We talked about what had transpired in the three minutes it took us to walk from our car into the church building and the eight seconds we had been standing in the foyer. The foyer was big and open which I love because I feel like I can easily scan the environment without worrying that I might miss something behind a wall. However, the number of people in the foyer overwhelmed me and, while I was trying to scan through a very large group of people, my husband walked away from me to throw something in the trash. Within seconds of being alone, I noticed someone I identified as a possible threat because of his size, something he was wearing, his lack of interaction with others, and because he was also scanning the room. Because my CTD developed within relationships, those old feelings of distrust are easily projected on the person relationally and emotionally closest to me during a trigger.

A third indication I have been triggered, which I wouldn't realize until years later, is fawning. Fawning, according to the dictionary, is the ability to display exaggerated flattery or affection. A few years ago, during a large group Bible study at church, a man walked in who was covered in tattoos, his ears were bent over and bulged in the back, and he walked a bit hunched over with his head down. He was an MMA fighter and everything about him looked scary. It scared me that he hunched in his chair not making eye contact with anyone even though he knew many people in the room. When I noticed him, I immediately turned to my husband and, in a regretful tone, said, "I'm gonna have to go over and say hi to this guy if I'm going to function at all in here." Understanding the situation, my husband very calmly said "Okay" and offered to come with me. I told him "No" and headed in that direction. I introduced myself to his wife, his family, and finally to him. I tried sparking up a conversation with him but he wouldn't look at me and his wife answered most of the questions. I didn't feel good about this. When it was time to head down to pick up our kids this dude was already down there to pick up his own kids. So, again I approached him and tried to make conversation. His answers were short and he kept his head down.

This interaction between us continued for two or three weeks before his wife and I found ourselves having coffee together with a group of mutual friends. As the group dwindled, his wife and I started a conversation that ended with her subtly questioning if I was hitting on her husband. I was so embarrassed. She said women never approach him because he looks too scary and, typically, most men also stay away from him. She voiced that she was surprised to learn that I was going out of my way to talk with him. I was mortified and quickly explained myself.

The conversation with this woman was the first time I recognized I was fawning. The need for me to make someone I'm afraid of feel good about themselves. This skill, although a manipulation tactic, helped me to manage my dad's anger. Some days flattering him or lightening his mood would keep him from becoming angry and some days it would reduce the anger. I've noticed more and more over the years that I will often greet men I am slightly concerned about with a side hug or go out of my way to make them laugh or lighten the mood. As I've contemplated this, I've wondered how many men or their wives thought I was flirting. I also wonder how many women in general don't recognize that they are fawning and end up getting themselves into unsafe or unhealthy situations when their intent was to avoid one. I am learning that this behavior, which once served me, is now leading me to approach people my internal radar is telling me to run from. This is something I'm still working on.

The last, and for me, most important indication of a trigger, is a sick feeling in my stomach after an interaction with someone. This feeling usually alerts me to a relational trigger and is very important for me to address in order to maintain relationships. I have learned over the years that this feeling is typically caused by someone else's lack of boundaries or by my own lack of boundaries. Because boundaries are what keep me feeling safe in a relationship, when I don't hold to them or someone else doesn't hold to them, I am triggered and the relationship becomes untrustworthy.

**Task three:**

My therapist communicated that without a paradigm shift from CTD being a liability to an asset, I may never get to a point where CTD doesn't own me in some way. To take back control, I would need to see CTD as an asset. My therapist, who had a gentle sense of humor, without glorifying or giving me more credit than I deserved or a false sense of heroism, encouraged me to start recognizing that I had Jason Bourne skills. She explained that many people, specifically people in the military and first responders, are trained to do things I do naturally. She encouraged me to see my hypervigilance as an asset and to recognize the benefit this could be to my family. She joked that I basically live with a superpower and the best thing I can do for myself and my family is to harness that superpower for good purposes. Keeping my son and daughter safe is a good purpose. Keeping unknown children safe at the same event as me is a good purpose. Keeping my family safe is a good purpose. And keeping me safe is a good purpose.

The Bible shares a story about a man named Joseph who is despised by his brothers. Joseph's brothers sell him into slavery. As I read about the heartbreaking choices of Joseph's brothers, which affect Joseph for the rest of his life, and I ponder the evil in it, it's remarkable that the story ends with God using his brothers' evil for good. God first uses Joseph's suffering to provide food for Joseph's family during a famine. Then He uses Joseph's suffering to provide food for the entire Israelite community, who otherwise would have died. Joseph's brothers intended for Joseph to remain an Egyptian slave, but God used Joseph as an asset. Joseph's suffering was used to protect his family initially but, later, the entire people of Israel. At the end of this story, Joseph says to his brothers, "You intended to harm me, but God intended it for good to accomplish what is now being done, the saving of many lives." (Gen 50:20, NIV)

I had to work toward acknowledging that CTD is one way God protected me. CTD was a gift, it was God's grace in my life. It helped keep me alive, at best, and minimized some of the beatings, at the least.

I wish I didn't live with CTD. I wish I wasn't abused as a child. But I know that God will use my suffering to bring about good. Because of my suffering, I am an advocate for my children. I am more aware of people who are unhealthy, and I am more interested in my children's safety than in not offending someone. I'm unsure how God will use my story, but if even one person is helped by this book, then God used my circumstances for good.

# Ponder

Consider pondering the following questions. To be gentle with yourself, I suggest pondering one set of questions a day, being as honest as possible. Have empathy for yourself in this process.

Are your coping mechanisms still serving you or have you found that they now own you? How?

Are you managing your trauma alone? If so, is there someone you trust enough that you would be willing to share your story with them? Can you include your partner by sharing some of your coping mechanisms?

Have you been able to make a paradigm shift? Do you see your CTD as an asset or a liability?

Are you able to identify anything in your circumstances that God has used for good?

# Part II

# The Old

This house, harboring the old,
greedy, selfish, angry, wounded liars.
Watches, as a relentless Spirit dances about.
His movements collect the brokenness,
His grace, constant.
The doors slam, the walls shake, some days
the air has a stench.
But with every change in formation the Spirit shouts,
He urges, He insists:
*Do not wage war as humans do.*
*Be obedient. Take every thought captive.*
*Meditate on the King's truth, dwelling in honorable thoughts*
*Be lovely as you are.*
Every moment you are lovely, every healed wound, every drop of sweat,
every tear that moves the old toward the lovely new is a "fuck you" to the
enemy and a "come and see what God has done."

# Chapter Ten
## My Marriage and Attachment

*Suffering is a given; suffering alone is intolerable* - Author Unknown

"Children can't be witnesses." That's what the cop said when my mom called for help after her boyfriend beat her up while we watched. It was her word against his. She had no marks on her body and her boyfriend left before the cops arrived.

Because there was nothing the cops could immediately do for us, because there were no "witnesses," I watched my mom, after the initial letdown of not being protected, walk back into the house, smoke a cigarette to help her calm down, and then prepare herself for her boyfriend's return. She had to steal herself to disregard the beating so she could "live" as many days or hours or minutes as possible without another beating.

Once I moved in with my dad, this type of "living" would become normal for me as well. Every day I would put on the face, project the mood or show the interest that would be most pleasing to him, to minimize the anger, the beatings, and the rage.

Although I couldn't be considered a witness, I carried every memory, every trigger, and my stripped sense of self into my marriage.

As a young adult, my life lacked a deep understanding of a healthy marriage. My understanding of how adults functioned in relationships consisted of meth addiction, alcoholism, marijuana dependence, women being afraid of the men they lived with, neglect, and various forms of physical, verbal, sexual, and emotional abuse. So, I never planned on getting married. I dated often but, after only one or two dates, I moved on, knowing that I never planned to marry or put myself in a situation where I could get pregnant. That is, until my senior year of college when I met my future husband.

My husband, Ezra, with both his health and his dysfunction, was custom-made, perfect for me. Jesus knew we would be great for each other, as iron sharpens iron. Ezra loved Jesus and was extremely good-looking, stable, adventurous, fun, hard-working, intelligent, and *emotionally unavailable*. I hadn't met anyone like him before. He lacked both emotional highs and lows, which made him feel very safe to me. My husband's reactions to good and bad were so reasonable that I often described him as being "flat-lined" emotionally. To be clear, my husband was happy a lot of the time, but the joke in our house quickly became, *don't forget to tell your face you're happy!* The only exception to this was when we traveled which brought out some excitement and a sense of awe and wonder for him and he would express it. To be married to someone whose emotions never ran high or low was the safest, most comforting relationship I could have asked for.

Ezra and I hadn't been married long, maybe a couple of months. We had sex on the brain and Ezra said something to try to get me into bed. I reacted by playfully running around to the other side of our bed waiting for him to chase me. As he lunged forward to start his efforts, I jumped up onto the bed, ran as fast as I could across our California king, and jumped down to the other side. Catching up to me, Ezra reached out, touching the top of my shoulder. The joy I felt immediately left me and fear overcame me. I burst into a weeping, shaking mess. Ezra, with concern in his eyes, asked what was wrong and if I was okay. When I didn't respond, he sat next to me on the bed while I wept. When I was finally ready to speak, I told him that the chasing scared me and I wasn't sure he wouldn't hurt me. I could see the hurt in his eyes.

While writing this chapter, my husband and I celebrated our twentieth wedding anniversary. It's honestly a miracle that we've lasted this long since divorce or me leaving him was consistently on the table during our first fifteen years of marriage. It wasn't that I didn't love him. For me, over those fifteen years, love was not a feeling but a choice and an action. To not leave him was my choice to love. However, the freedom I felt in the threat to divorce him reinforced that I was still safe; that my husband couldn't lock the door behind me. Threatening divorce, and experiencing his safe reaction to my threat helped me feel safe enough to continue choosing to stay.

A friend with a history of abuse once told me that, in his marriage, he lives with one foot out the door. After pondering this statement, I concluded that this wasn't how my marriage worked. I was always all-in, both feet planted firmly in the marriage...until I was triggered. The moment I became triggered, the fear I felt was so great that running felt like my only option. What I've learned over the years is that I have a difficult time processing my fear or a trigger when my husband is present, specifically if he is the source of the trigger. Therefore, the idea of packing my bags or divorcing him seemed like the only possible options for dealing with whatever issue we were having.

Now, you might automatically assume that in the relationship I am an avoider of conflict, or I need time alone to process. Not true. I'm not afraid of conflict; I'm particularly strong-willed, and opinionated, and honestly, I like a good fight and can be aggressive. In an argument, I have to watch my mouth; my husband has set his boundary that if I drop an f-bomb he will not continue the conversation with me. So, not only did I not understand what was happening to me in times when I wanted to flee, but I also could not explain to my husband what was happening to me.

My understanding changed when I read the book *The Deepest Well* by Nadine Burke Harris, M.D. In it, Harris paints a picture of what is happening internally for a person with trauma. She sets up the following scenario...

In order for humans to survive, the brain and body had to come up with efficient ways of processing information, and the stress-response system is one of them. If a little kid touches a hot stove, his body remembers. Biochemically, it tags or bookmarks the stove (and all the stimuli associated with it) as being dangerous, so the next time the boy sees someone turning on the burners, his body sends him all kinds of warning signs: vivid memories, muscle tension, and rapid pulse. Usually, this is enough to dissuade him from doing the same thing again. In this way, our bodies are trying to protect us, which makes a lot of sense...

But the stress response can do its job a little too well sometimes. This happens when the response to stimuli goes from adaptive and lifesaving to maladaptive and health-damaging. For example, almost everyone knows that soldiers sometimes come back from the front lines with post-traumatic stress disorder. This condition is an extreme example of the body remembering too much. With

PTSD THE STRESS RESPONSE REPEATEDLY CONFUSES CURRENT
STIMULI WITH THE PAST IN SUCH A DRAMATIC WAY THAT IT BE-
COMES HARD FOR THESE VETS TO LIVE IN THE PRESENT. WHETHER
IT'S A B-52 BOMBER IN THE SKY OR A COMMERCIAL AIRLINE OVER-
HEAD TAKING TOURISTS TO HAWAII, THEIR BODIES FEEL THE
SAME-*IN MORTAL DANGER*. THE PROBLEM WITH PTSD IS THAT IT
BECOMES ENTRENCHED; THE STRESS RESPONSE IS CAUGHT IN THE
PAST, STUCK ON REPEAT.

Because my trauma was interpersonal, I am triggered by relational interactions. In the same way the military vet is triggered by an airplane, I can
be triggered by a facial expression, a comment, a movement, an inconsistency in a relationship, etc. Relationships for me can be confusing and
processing through a trigger can take time because my body remembers
when my brain is not making the connection.

Harris further explains, "The body senses danger, and it sets off a
firestorm of chemical reactions aimed to protect itself. But most important, *the body remembers*. ...We all have a stress-response system, and it is
carefully calibrated and highly individualized by both genetics and early
experiences."

Unfortunately, my stress-response system has been calibrated to protect me from the people in my life closest to me. For me to explain the
implications of this to my husband, to help him understand my desire to
flee, I used Harris' explanation about bears:

ESSENTIALLY, IT WORKS LIKE THIS: IMAGINE, YOU'RE WALKING
IN THE FOREST AND YOU SEE A BEAR. IMMEDIATELY, YOUR BRAIN
SENDS A BUNCH OF SIGNALS TO YOUR ADRENAL GLANDS ...SAYING,
*"RELEASE STRESS HORMONES! ADRENALINE! CORTISOL!"* SO, YOUR
HEART STARTS TO POUND, YOUR PUPILS DILATE, YOUR AIRWAY

OPENS UP, AND YOU ARE READY TO EITHER FIGHT THE BEAR OR RUN
FROM THE BEAR.

Harris goes on to explain how a person's entire system works together
to give a person what he/she needs to survive the bear attack. She talks
about how our stress response system adjusts within seconds to minutes
for survival purposes. She goes on to explain that once we get away from
the bear, our stress-response system settles.

The problem for people with CTD is that their stress response systems
do not shut down, but rather, run around the clock. Growing up I never
experienced getting away from the bear because the bear lived in my
house with me.

Harris eventually asks a question that helped me organize the chaos
of what was happening to me when arguing with my husband. "What
happens when you can't experience safety in your cave because the bear
is living in the cave with you?" This metaphor in the form of a question
was extremely helpful in understanding myself.

Now, when my husband does something seemingly inconsequential
to him but terrifying to me, I can tell him that there is a bear in my cave.
This indicates to him that I've been triggered – something he's done,
maybe a comment, a little white lie, a facial expression, irritability or
simply a movement has signaled to my body to be afraid.

Let me give you an example. I come down to the kitchen after getting
ready for church and my husband says, "Wow, you look beautiful."
Then, as I'm making myself a cup of coffee he says, "You look a little
tired, why don't you sit down and drink your coffee and I'll make breakfast?" That's a guaranteed trigger. Anything that looks remotely like
inconsistency *first I look beautiful, then I look tired* prompts my body to
prepare to protect itself. Growing up it was common for my dad to make
a statement to someone in public that suggested he was proud of me

and then call me a fucking idiot when we got into the house indicating the beginning stages of a rage. Or, he would say we had no money so I wouldn't ask for necessities like deodorant or a working toilet, but then he'd drive through Taco Bell for dinner when we already had food in the refrigerator.

Although it's reasonable for me to be triggered by something related to my past experiences, it's not reasonable for my husband to be held accountable for something that should be totally normal in relationships. His comments about me being beautiful and tired are not actually inconsistencies; I can be *both* beautiful and tired. There is no meanness in these two true statements and they have never indicated the beginning stage of a rage for my husband however, my body is responding to what it remembers.

The problem for years was that my body was reacting to a bear in my cave because my body was remembering, but my brain wasn't making sense of my body's response to the interaction. My kind husband is making me breakfast. Why am I so angry? Why do I want to leave? Why do I feel like divorce is my only option in this situation? I found that it took me being alone or at least distancing myself from the trigger or "the bear" for many hours before I could feel safe again. Once safe I could truly process the issue. Identifying the *past issue* and acknowledging the *present trigger* are the initial steps to repairing my relationship with my husband and moving from fear and anger into *connection*.

Because of my new understanding, divorce and leaving my husband is largely off the table. I say largely because I am still a work in progress. It is more common now for me to start by saying, "There's a bear in my cave" than to say, "I want a divorce." And it has been very helpful for my husband to understand the complexity of the situation when I say: "The inconsistency I *felt* in your words triggered me. Thanks for saying I look beautiful, thanks for recognizing that I'm tired, and thanks for making breakfast." He is now able to accept my apology and love me despite my crazy *wink.

On a side note, I've found it significantly easier to initiate the need for space rather than threaten divorce when I take really good care of my nervous system (stress response system). I address this in the next chapter.

## Attachment

Now, you might be thinking that my husband must loathe being married to me and maybe even hides from me. However, this is not the case. We actually have a lot of fun and share a lot of joy. We work well together. For the first fifteen years, we had a partnership, business-like, with lots of sex, lots of fun, and lots of Jesus. We did a lot of work to better understand both our dysfunctions and were able to create interactional norms that benefited both of us. However, the closer I grew to my husband the more recognizable it became that something between us was missing.

Throughout our fostering journey, we took classes on attachment; we were asked to learn about attachment styles to help the children in our home attach to us. More specifically, we were being asked, during times of conflict, to move toward our son to meet his needs so he could attach to us. I felt frustrated after every therapy session. I would walk out feeling like I didn't understand what the therapist was asking me to do or how to apply it. But after reflecting, I realized that this was the very element missing in my marriage. I didn't feel attached and wasn't sure how to make it happen.

Dr. Sue Johnson, a clinical psychologist and primary developer of Emotionally Focused Therapy, known for her work in adult attachments, bonding, and romantic relationships, concludes in her book, *Hold Me Tight*, that love and attachment are actually needed for survival. Based on the results of several research studies, attachment, and secure connection is essential for every part of our physical, mental, and emotional health. Healthy, positive, and secure attachments are shown to control high blood pressure, reduce stress hormones, lower the risk of heart attack, and reduce both physical and mental pain. Having healthy, positive, and secure attachments makes the immune system stronger, supports the human body in healing itself from physical trauma, and helps to regulate the brain. Dr. Johnson points to a study conducted by Israeli researchers: "Couples with secure emotional attachment are much more able to deal with dangers such as Scud missile attacks than other less-connected couples. They are less anxious and have fewer physical problems after attacks."

I found this research interesting because Dr. Harris, in her book *The Deepest Well,* reports that prolonged activation of a person's stress-response system weakens the immune system, raises blood pressure, increases the chance of a heart attack, and elevates stress hormones. A person with what Harris labels *toxic stress* typically has a shorter life span and the toxic stress triggers health problems. Harris states,

TOXIC STRESS RESPONSE CAN OCCUR WHEN A CHILD EXPERIENCES STRONG, FREQUENT, AND/OR PROLONGED ADVERSITY – SUCH AS PHYSICAL OR EMOTIONAL ABUSE, NEGLECT, CAREGIVER SUBSTANCE ABUSE OR MENTAL ILLNESS, EXPOSURE TO VIOLENCE, AND/OR THE ACCUMULATED BURDENS OF FAMILY ECONOMIC HARDSHIP— WITHOUT ADEQUATE ADULT SUPPORT. THIS KIND OF PROLONGED ACTIVATION OF THE STRESS-RESPONSE SYSTEM CAN

DISRUPT THE DEVELOPMENT OF BRAIN ARCHITECTURE AND OTH-
ER ORGAN SYSTEMS, AND INCREASE THE RISK FOR STRESS-RELAT-
ED DISEASE AND COGNITIVE IMPAIRMENT, WELL INTO THE ADULT
YEARS.

The conclusion I reached after reading these two books was in order to heal I had to attach and allow myself to be loved. But, how?

For our twentieth wedding anniversary, my husband suggested we take a trip to Turks and Caicos while I suggested we do a marriage-intensive retreat based in Emotionally Focused Therapy. His response to me was, "I'm 100% in." I don't need to tell you that sitting with a therapist for five hours a day was not as fun as Turks and Caicos, but it was totally worth it!

According to The International Centre for Excellence in Emotionally Focused Therapy (ICEEFT), Emotionally Focused Therapy (EFT) is a humanistic approach to psychotherapy developed in tandem with the science of adult attachment, a profound developmental theory of personality and intimate relationships. During our time with our therapist, she helped us see how conflict is actually an opportunity for connection and attachment. She reviewed with us how children attach to their parents. When babies are in distress or have needs, they cry. When the caregiver provides what the baby needs (a diaper change, food, a hug), the baby calms down, and attachment is developed. The child builds a bond with the caregiver based on the child getting its needs met. Providing for the child's needs helps the child regulate their emotions, develop a sense of self and value, and teaches the child empathy.

Our therapist helped us understand that adult intimate relationships work the same way. This means when we have conflict with each other, the conflict is an opportunity to either flee and live in old patterns or to connect and bond over finding a solution to the conflict, having empathy for each other, and meeting each other's needs. Our therapist helped us to see our negative cycle while trying to reach resolution and helped us create a new positive cycle.

Our therapist also taught us ways to build trust before conflict happens. Distrust and triggers are obstacles for me, keeping me from bonding and being able to connect in conflict. Learning this, our therapist gave us trust exercises to do together throughout the week, and, no, trust falls are not included. The exercises helped us build trust in a peaceful time so when conflict inevitably arises, my body remembers the trust-building interactions allowing my nervous system to stay calm at the beginning of conflict, allowing us to move directly into connecting and bonding. This might sound silly to people who trust and attach to others easily, but for me this was groundbreaking. For the first time in my life, I am starting to feel attached to my husband, the person closest to me, which is profound and life-giving.

My husband, who says that he has always felt attached to me, has communicated that having me more bonded and attached to him has created a significant shift in our marriage. With me attached, he feels our relationship is easier, deeper, and more stable.

I honestly don't think I could have stayed married to my husband or been willing to do trust exercises if I didn't have God to anchor to over the years. On really tough days, when triggers and distrust owned me, God was the only refuge I had. If you struggle to attach and you're not ready for this level of trust and bonding yet, take your time. I'm just now working through it, limping along. But, "limping along" is still progress even if it's small and slow. On days when I need a great big inhale and a safe place to exhale, I spend time with God.

"Come to me, all you who are weary and burdened, and I will give you rest. Take my yoke upon you and learn from me, for I am gentle and humble in heart, and you will find rest for your souls. For my yoke is easy and my burden is light." (Matthew 11:28-30, NIV)

# Ponder

Consider pondering the following questions. To be gentle with yourself, I suggest pondering one set of questions a day, being as honest as possible. Have empathy for yourself in this process.

Sometimes our stress response system engages because there truly is an unsafe person in our *cave*. The following questions do not apply to relationships with unsafe people.

Disconnection and survival are not living. Do you ever feel, when interacting with others who are safe, like there's a "bear in your cave"? If so, how often do you feel this way? How often are you ready to fight, fidget, freeze, fawn, or run from them?

We were created and designed for connection. Do you feel attached and are you living a relationally connected life? If so, with whom are you connected? Is this a healthy connection? Why or why not?

Are there times when your body's reaction to a situation doesn't make sense to you? List some of those situations and the confusion around those situations.

Have you ever considered conflict an opportunity for attachment?

# Chapter Eleven

## My Children and My Motherhood

*Love is not affectionate feeling, but a steady wish for the loved person's ultimate good as far as it can be obtained -* CS Lewis

My newborn baby's screaming, her crying, her fussing for her needs to be met was one of the most triggering experiences of my adult life. I would meet her needs as soon as possible – not to love her, but to make the screaming stop. I was attentive to my own survival, not hers. My attentiveness created, for her, an attachment to me. However, her vulnerable, newborn cry, sent my stress response system into go mode. I didn't know it then, but my body was responding as if I was living with a bear in my cave – a bear I needed to protect, nurture and provide for all while trying to navigate triggers so pervasive there was absolutely no way for me to attach to her. It was all I could do to just stay; it was a heroic feat to not run or leave her and yet so basic it's embarrassing and heartbreaking. My husband was capable and loving; without his presence, I don't know if I would have stayed.

The only time I felt like I was attaching was when I was breastfeeding. I don't know the physiological explanation for this, but I'm guessing it had something to do with the positive hormones pumping through me while nursing. However, when I wasn't nursing, in order to stay, I would sometimes picture how my life might have been different if *my* mother had stayed. I wondered what my life would have been like had my own mother known Jesus or thought she was capable enough to care for me.

Wanting the ultimate good for my daughter, I stayed. I had hoped that staying would communicate that I wanted her, that she was worth the fight.

Because attaching was difficult for me, "Fake it 'till you make it" has been my motto in motherhood. Observation and an adult game of copycat are how I've been successful in treating my children how they deserve to be treated. For example, I observed a friend greet her toddler at eye level, showering her with kisses and hugs, then sitting with her, telling her all the things she loved about her. So, with my daughter, I did the same. I listened to my mother-in-law call my daughter "Love." She'd say, "Come here Love, let me help you." So, I did the same. I watched Ella, my grafted mom, know her children's likes and dislikes and then provide them with things they liked so, I did the same. My education and career as a teacher taught me how to encourage and set boundaries, be consistent with children by creating routines, providing options, and giving praise for hard work. I wasn't attached to my students but I was still considered a loved teacher, so I applied this approach to my children.

My ability to fawn has often, in my motherhood, been a saving grace. There have been numerous times I've interacted with my children while being triggered. After some of these interactions, I've asked my husband, "Did I come across angry or upset? Because internally I was losing my shit" To which he would usually respond, "No, you looked fine, like nothing was wrong." Although always relieved to hear this, I've known that my children pick up on the subtleties of my CTD even when I'm fawning. My children will say "Mom, tell me what I just said. I'm talking to you, but I know you're thinking of something else." They recognize my lack of presence and often recognize when I'm trying to hide a trigger response.

Over the years my kids have also begun to show that they have adapted to some of my trigger responses. For example, if they drop and break a plate or they trip and fall without injury they will immediately say, "I'm okay", knowing that if I think they are wounded, my extreme startle response will cause me to jump up, run to them, and often become angry over metaphorical spilled milk.

Out of fear that my children will go bankrupt paying off therapy bills, I have tried to be as open and honest about my CTD as possible. Since I haven't found a children's book directly addressing CTD, I read a book called *Why are you so scared? A Child's Book About Parents With PTSD* by Beth Andrews. This book has helped my children understand what is happening to me during a trigger. I feel this is important so that my children don't think they've done something wrong. I want my children to understand that my behaviors are not their fault and are not caused by them.

Sometimes when triggered, anger surfaces because my body goes into fight mode. The most important thing I can do when this happens is repair the damage I've caused by allowing my children to watch me apologize to my husband or by directly apologizing to them. For my kids, the repairing process allows me to own my mistake and its effect on them as well as teach them, that my anger wasn't their fault.

My triggers have always felt more intense around my children. So, when I didn't understand how an outing to the playground would turn into hours of sleep, my psychologist explained that my nervous system —stress response system—doesn't have a braking mechanism. It is either completely on, preparing for danger or death, or it is off (which, for me, I think means I'm unconscious *wink). So, my experience in watching my little girl trip and fall on the playground, even though after a short cry, she would get up, dust herself off and continue playing, produced the same intensity as if I watched her get hit by a car. The intensity in the metaphor of *watching my daughter get hit by a car* was exactly what I felt in seemingly trivial situations like a scraped knee or crying over the loss of a stuffed animal.

The thing with kids is that they are much less predictable than the average adult. They fall easily, cry unexpectedly, need lots of undivided attention, and throw tantrums for tiny unmet expectations. The triggers for me were endless, making motherhood completely exhausting, almost unmanageable. However, once I understood the role my nervous system (stress response system) plays in my trigger responses, I decided the best thing I could do for myself and my family was to heal and support my nervous system. Over the years, I've experimented with various strategies to support my nervous system resulting in my current lifestyle. The strategies I currently use allow me to live in states of abandon where I can attach.

Currently, I eat a (mostly) anti-inflammatory and low-refined sugar diet. I take a multivitamin that regulates my blood sugar so that it doesn't drop too low. I've completed a prescribed treatment plan from a functional-medicine doctor that helped heal and support my endocrine system. I've also worked with my general practitioner and read *The Mood Cure: The 4-Step Program to Take Charge of Your Emotions Today* by Julia Ross to address specific concerns regarding trauma-induced stress and depression. As a result, I currently take an amino acid regimen that includes GABA: Gamma-Aminobutyric Acid. Though I've had success with amino acids, after reading *The Deepest Well*,

I'm now researching a medication called guanfacine, which is a doctor-prescribed medication that targets the frontal lobe of the brain.

Environmentally, I get eight-to-ten hours of sleep a night. I can't emphasize enough the importance of sleep. If I'm tired, I'm triggered significantly easier and more often. I don't watch the news or scary shows and I try to avoid mystery books or books on war because they remind me of the ugliness in the world. I can become hypervigilant for days or weeks after an interaction with one of these resources. I take self-defense classes and exercise regularly. The research on the benefits of exercise is incredible and I feel the most calm and grounded after I exercise. I limit relationships with people I don't intrinsically trust and I set safety limits for my children (e.g., sleepovers, playdates, curfews, and dating). I have created an environment in my home that also supports my nervous system. Our home's colors, layout, organization, alarm systems, and rules all help to keep my nervous system under control so I can enjoy my family.

Pre-planning also plays a major role in managing my nervous system. I create plans that are healthy for perceived threats. For example, when I walk into a restaurant, I choose a seat that allows me to see the entrance to the building and, if possible, a seat that allows me to have my back against a wall. When I go to a workout, I identify a person in the room who seems vigilant. I place myself opposite this person so when my back is to a door during a workout, I can simply look up to read that person's face. Additionally, I choose smaller venues for activities like pumpkin or apple picking and I try to avoid crowds whenever possible. I sometimes prepare for going out by doing a self-care activity (i.e., anything that makes me feel calm, like painting, writing, worshiping, or napping).

Lastly, I do my best to stay grounded in Scripture and to rest in, and with, the Holy Spirit. On my website, you will find a free grounding exercise I use called *Anchored*. There were years when I used this exercise upwards of ten times a day. Today, since I'm able to stay grounded longer, I either don't need this exercise at all or, based on my need, pick and choose portions of the exercise to use. I've had people encourage me to read my Bible daily and, though I'm sure this is a fantastic habit for some people, it just doesn't work for me. I find that it's better for me to be involved in a Bible study group for accountability or read the Bible on my own once a week. Then, I meditate on that one reading throughout the week to absorb it, believe it, and trust it. Most importantly for me, I spend a lot of time in worship and prayer. I don't know why, but worship is extremely comforting to me. I think it's because during worship I'm focused and meditating on God's character and attributes.

Once my nervous system was supported, I began experiencing moments, and sometimes hours, of what I call *abandon*. Abandon for me is life without hypervigilance, triggers, and fear. Moments of abandon are opportunities for me to create good memories and attachments with my children. They are moments when I am fully present and able to respond to my children's needs in ways they feel connected – and I feel connected, which allows me to attach to them.

Once I started having moments of abandon, I began partnering with my family to help extend these moments into hours and days. For example, typically after 7:00 pm, I'm exhausted – aren't most moms? My children know, and I remind them, "It's 7:00 pm and I'm tired so the best thing for all of us is to just be chill." I recognize that my kids have to steal themselves to keep from arguing with each other or discussing emotional matters with me. I sometimes feel like I'm not a good mom because I have to ask my children to partner with me in order for me to avoid being triggered –they're children and this shouldn't be their responsibility.

However, asking them to partner with me helps me to live in longer periods of abandon, which allows me to have healthy attachment and connection with them. It allows me to be a better version of myself, which I think they will appreciate later in life.

Another way of partnering with my family is handing over to my husband responsibilities that most people would traditionally consider a mother's role. For example, my husband takes the kids to their dentist and doctor appointments because a little blood or my kids crying from a vaccine shot sends my nervous system into go mode. When my kids come home from getting a shot at the doctor's office, I can give hugs and be empathetic while they share their feelings and I share mine (e.g., how painful it was, how much I love them, how sad I am for them, and how I'm proud of them). My husband and I agree that anything that could lead to blood or bruising is not a healthy activity for me to do with my kids unless he is around to manage the potential wounds and screaming.

For me, abandon is needed for attachment, and attachment is needed for a healthy relationship with my children. I do the work to support my nervous system so I can attach.

I've really struggled emotionally while writing this chapter because I feel sad for my kids, that they didn't get a mentally healthier mom. However, I keep hearing the words, "Don't talk about my daughter that way." I once heard a speaker at a women's event at my church say that when her daughter says something negative about herself, this woman likes to say to her daughter, "Don't talk about my daughter that way." The speaker connected this concept to our relationship with God. Now, when I feel like tearing myself apart because I think I'm not a good enough mom, God, who knows where I've been and Who understands that I'm doing my best, gives me, through the Holy Spirit, the words ...

"Don't talk about my daughter that way."

In the wake of my abuse, I have deficiencies that I have to acknowledge. I also have to acknowledge that I currently struggle and will always struggle with the tendency to manage my deficiencies based on *my* definition of good. My definition of good, in my motherhood, was to stay even when attaching was an unfathomable thought. Staying without attachment is not what God considers good. Even when I'm doing my very best brokenness still exists.

And yet, God calls me Beloved.

Not only does He call me Beloved, but He continues to heal me, teaching me how to attach while loving me throughout the process.

Maybe you haven't had support – no healthy family to lean on, and no capable or loving partner, and in your distress and in the wake of your abuse you felt, in your own definition of good, the best way you could love your babies was to give them up for adoption, leave them at a firehouse or hospital, or abort them. Please know that God sees what you've been through, He sees your internal struggle, and He calls you Beloved. He will heal you, mending all the broken parts, and, in the process, He will show you love.

If you're doing your best to love your babies but you feel like you're crawling out of your skin and so exhausted that it's hard to function, you're not alone. If the best way you can love your babies is to just stay, to show up knowing you have nothing else to give, God knows what you've been through, He knows your internal struggle and He calls you Beloved. He will heal you, mending all the broken parts, and, in the process, He will show you love.

If there is guilt or shame because of what you lack as a mother or because of the choices you've made as a mother, God sees you and His

Grace is sufficient for you and your babies. Despite what you lack, you're an image-bearer.

God calls you Beloved.

# Ponder

Consider pondering the following questions. To be gentle with yourself, I suggest pondering one set of questions a day, being as honest as possible. Have empathy for yourself in this process.

Reflect on the situations that bring anger when parenting. Write a list of these situations. Are any of these situations associated with a trigger?

How often do you tear yourself down or assume you're not doing a good enough job as a parent? Since tearing yourself down doesn't help your parenting, write a list of the things you're doing well.

Write a couple of small goals that will help you work toward healthy relationships with your children. Change starts with one small goal at a time.

Do you carry grief, sadness, or shame because you chose not to stay or keep your children? Do you believe that despite your inability, God's love for you and His desire for your ultimate good still exists? Have you considered praying for your children who are being raised by others, knowing that God's grace is sufficient for them?

If your mother or your father did not stay, God is grieved for you. Babies being separated from their parents is not God's design, it's not His ultimate good. Are you able to grieve for yourself?

You may have had the most amazing upbringing, having been adopted by another family. Do you believe this was the grace of God in your life?

Do you feel attached to your children? If so, what does attachment look like for you? If not, how do you feel in the absence of attachment?

Is there something you can change in your life that could help support your nervous system –stress response system?

I can often be sad that my children did not get a mentally healthier mom. However, when they throw attitude about what we're having for dinner or ask if we can stop at Starbucks on the way home or are mad because they have to clean their rooms, I am reminded that my children's ability to talk back, throw attitude, ask for what they want, and complain means I've created *safety*. It means they aren't afraid of me. It means that, in our home, they don't know hunger or abuse and this is when I know I'm winning. Despite my failures and all that I lack, my children will be the first generation in my family to not grow up in an abusive home. This is something to celebrate. List, despite what you lack, all the things you can celebrate in your own family.

# Chapter Twelve

## Community and Family

*To believe, and to consent to be
loved while unworthy, is the great
secret.* - Wm. R. Newell

I was sitting on the toilet seat watching as my mom put on her makeup. She was so beautiful. I'd watch her get ready until the man she was dating, who seemed to be kind, came to the door to pick her up. I once asked my mother why she didn't keep dating that kind man. She said, "Because I didn't think I was good enough."

The day my dad was arrested I had been living with Ruth and her family for about a week. Her parents, Michael and Ella Pederson, were planning on celebrating their twentieth wedding anniversary that evening. After the news about my dad, they canceled their plans to stay home with me. It wouldn't be until years later, after processing their generosity, that I would understand the significance of what they did. They forfeited their twentieth wedding anniversary celebration to be with me—not to talk about it, not to process it, unless I wanted to—just to be with me.

They stayed home so I wouldn't be alone.

Although I was oblivious to my need for community. It was this kind of community that helped me survive. I needed a community to heal in, to grow in, and to rest in. I once read somewhere that abuse happens within human relationships; therefore, healing and trust need to be restored, not alone, but within human relationships. Michael and Ella, being *with me*, and allowing me to live in their home, gave me an opportunity to observe a family function in a way I hadn't experienced before.

Over the years, each community I belonged to and every relationship I was in that *reflected God's good*, allowed me, by simply being with me and including me, to observe ways of living I hadn't experienced before. I was able to observe others being patient with each other when they were frustrated. I was able to observe people forgive each other, implement boundaries, and have standards that *reflected God's good*. Community allowed me to interact with people who were unafraid of the world, helping me to make connections by seeing the disconnect between their beliefs and mine about people and safety.

The biggest obstacle to being in community was my feeling of not being good enough. It was the same feeling that kept my mother from not experiencing kind relationships. Had I allowed my feelings and beliefs about myself to rule me, I would have never experienced the sacrifice of the single parent with three kids who drove me to work every day because I needed a ride. I wouldn't have gained two best friends, one who would eventually become my sister, who would wait for me after therapy sessions to sit with me while I cried. I wouldn't have relationships with multiple women in my life who would take the role of mama bear in different seasons. And I may not have married had I not built relationships with my college guy friends who showed me that young men could be safe. Each relationship I engaged in, even if the relationship went awry, was an opportunity for me to practice boundary-setting and trusting others and allowed me the space to start discovering my likes and dislikes.

In each community I've been a part of I've done my best to observe and learn, hoping that the new norms I was learning would help me create a different kind of life than I had growing up. For a long time, it felt difficult for me to set new norms because the gap between the life I knew and the life I wanted was too great to bridge. I didn't know how to bridge this gap without a clear sense of self so I spent a lot of time trying very hard to fit neatly into other people's way of living. What I've come to realize is the more focused I am on God's character and attributes and the more I reach out to Him to meet my needs, the clearer my identity and sense of self becomes. My sense of self, though under-defined compared to people without CTD, allows me to pick and choose my new norms. For example, once I was able to acknowledge that excessive drinking makes me feel uncomfortable and scared because it decreases my awareness leaving me to feel vulnerable *and my feelings mattered*, I was able to apply new norms for how to celebrate holidays and birthdays without the need to get drunk. Now, eating a good meal with people I love, traveling, or playing sports with friends are the ways I choose to celebrate.

In the process of healing from my abuse, I found that most of my life norms, the ways I lived that felt normal and healthy, were developed from unhealthy relationships and trauma-based environments. My norms were *not* actually healthy, *just comfortable*.

If you don't have CTD but love or care for someone who does, it is crucially important for you to just be present so they don't have to be alone if they don't want to be. When a person with CTD gets to be *with you*, they get the opportunity to observe and learn so they can determine what they believe, who they are, and how they want to behave.

FAITH ISN'T ABOUT KNOWING ALL OF THE RIGHT STUFF OR OBEY-ING A LIST OF RULES. IT'S SOMETHING MORE, SOMETHING MORE COSTLY BECAUSE IT INVOLVES BEING PRESENT AND MAKING A SAC-RIFICE. PERHAPS THAT'S WHY JESUS IS SOMETIMES CALLED IM-MANUEL – 'GOD WITH US.' I THINK THAT'S WHAT GOD HAD IN MIND, FOR JESUS TO BE PRESENT, TO JUST BE WITH US. IT'S ALSO WHAT HE HAS IN MIND FOR US WHEN IT COMES TO OTHER PEOPLE.
–BOB GOFF, *LOVE DOES*

If you have CTD and lack community because you struggle with the belief that you're not worthy, disgusting, or not good enough to belong, do everything you can to acknowledge that those thoughts and beliefs are *lies*. When focused on my thoughts about myself, I continually struggle with these feelings. When I focus on what God says about me as an image-bearer, my value is restored, making vulnerable engagement with others possible though still scary.

On my worst days, when I'm struggling with my worth and old mes-sages start drowning out what God says about me, I *ask* God for help. The conversation with God usually goes something like this:

"Hello Jesus, I feel like trash, I feel like the person my dad said I am, a fucking cunt." God has always been consistent in responding, "That's not your name. Hello, Beloved." He reminds me that I am an image-bearer, created to be in loving relationships and to help others heal, to maintain boundaries, and care for the things God cares for. I am dearly loved. I am chosen to belong to the kingdom of God. I am a child of God, adopted into His family. I am forgiven. I live in the presence of the Holy Spirit. I am a co-heir with Christ. I will never be abandoned but am sealed by the Holy Spirit. I belong to Jesus and my fate is secured by His sacrifice for me. God delights in me, my presence is enjoyed. The Lord God rejoices over me with gladness. He wants me in relationship with others and He wants a relationship with me.

If you're a follower of Jesus, this is also true for you. If you're not a follower of Jesus and you want to be, all you have to do is let Him in. He won't force His way into a relationship with you. He knocks as if your soul had a door, and He waits patiently and respectfully as you decide whether or not you want to invite Him in.

Opening that door is simply acknowledging that you *believe* in Him.

## Family

Community is imperative for growth; family is imperative for life lived abundantly.

The week before moving in with Ruth and her family I was dreading it. I knew her dad was a pastor and, knowing where I came from, I wasn't sure how I would fit into the household norms. The only saving grace in this situation was that Ruth, a sweet Christian girl with the best sense of humor and a mouth a little like a sailor, made me feel comfortable from the start of our friendship. I figured if I could feel comfortable with her, I might be comfortable with the rest of her family.

I spent the entire summer at the Pederson's house and I fit in just fine; I'm sure fawning helped with this. Over the next several years, the Pederson's would invite me back for every holiday and school vacation, even buying my plane tickets and finding me work before I got there.

I was given Christmas presents and included in family pictures. They communicated they were *with me* by inviting me, eating with me, and sitting with me night after night at the dinner table to discuss everything from big philosophical questions to seemingly insignificant occurrences in my day. There was no judgment expressed toward my questions or my answers. They constantly fed my soul with truth and perspective, encouraging me with words like "You're doing good, keep going." I never felt like a project. Their love and their generosity just were. They abided in it naturally because *they abide in Christ*.

I didn't know my boyfriend would one day ask Michael for my hand in marriage. I didn't know I would eventually call their sons "brothers," my best friend "sister," or that one day my children would call them "Grandma" and "Grandpa". I never would have imagined that I would eventually call them "mom" and "dad."

Communities and friendships come and go. Sometimes, if we're lucky, they last a lifetime, but the majority of the time they are in our lives for a season. The Pederson's, although they started as one of my communities, became my family; I was *grafted* in. The grafting wasn't easy.

Grafting, if you haven't had to do it, requires an immeasurable amount of change. Some of the change was glorious; I had a meal on the table every night, I had a mother who asked me my likes and dislikes and made decisions based on my answers, I had a safe dad and I was experiencing new and good norms. However, some of the grafting was painful as I had to grieve the loss of an entire family whose interpersonal abuse was too entangled to simply set boundaries with. I also had to set aside some of my cultural traditions and foods while I made sense of where I came from.

The Pedersons had to change their life around to make room for me and the Pederson's kids had to give up hours of time with their parents because I needed quite a lot of attention. There were hard days for both them and me. There were sacrifices, disagreements, misunderstandings, and lots of trust that needed to be built. But, there came a point when they were no longer my community – they were permanent, as much as humans can be.

Permanency allowed me to give love and experience love when being myself, *without* fawning. Permanency allowed me to experience what it means to stick it out, working through troubles and disagreements and choosing to love when sometimes I didn't feel like it.

As I've healed, my family has expanded. I have a relationship with my birth mom who has been clean for twenty years and I have varying degrees of relational closeness with a couple of my biological siblings and their spouses and children. I get to, out of my newly developed sense of self decide if I want to introduce my children and husband to the traditions and foods that come from my culture. I get to blend new traditions with my old traditions and start new traditions and norms with my birth family members I have relationships with. I get to do this because of *permanency*. I have been able to heal because of consistent permanent relationships, because of *family*.

Permanent relationships are those relationships that force us to keep growing, loving, and accepting love. If you've had to separate yourself from your family because of abuse and you don't have a grafted family, then let your community fulfill that need. I do find it important to understand the difference between a shifting, fluctuating community and the permanence of family. Knowing the difference has helped me organize feelings of abandonment and shift my perspective on permanent versus sometimes changing relationships.

If community and family are hard for you, let God be your permanence. He is the only one who is truly not going anywhere.

For I am convinced that neither death nor life, neither angels nor demons, neither the present nor the future, nor any powers, neither height nor depth, nor anything else in all creation, will be able to separate us from the love of God that is in Christ Jesus our Lord. (Romans 8:38-39, NIV)

God has always wanted you. He wants you grafted into *His* family. The grafting into God's family sometimes isn't easy, at least it wasn't for me. There were hard days, especially in the beginning. There will be sacrifices, disagreements, misunderstandings, and lots of trust that needs to be built between you and God. But, once you have settled and accepted you're a child of God, permanency will allow you to give love and experience love when being yourself. Permanency with God will allow you to experience love, acceptance, and belonging forever.

# Ponder

Consider pondering the following questions. To be gentle with yourself, I suggest pondering one set of questions a day, being as honest as possible. Have empathy for yourself in this process.

Do your feelings of not being good enough keep you from good things or good people?

New situations and circumstances are uncomfortable and scary. You're likely comfortable with what you're already familiar with.

What norms feel comfortable? Would God consider these norms good?

"Because abuse happens within human relationships, the effects of abuse are healed within human relationships" (unknown author). Do you have anyone in your life safe enough to be in community with? Do you believe God can heal you through a healthy community?

Who in your life is permanent? Are these permanent relationships safe and healthy? Do these relationships need boundaries?

Have you decided whether or not you want a relationship with God? Why or why not?

# Chapter Thirteen
## The Church

*The day we find the perfect church, it becomes imperfect the moment we join it.* - Charles H. Spurgeon

I was created to love my dad; therefore, I was willing to forgive and reconcile; all I required of him was to say he was sorry, and to take ownership. I was hopeful when I heard his voice on the other end of the phone telling me after he had been arrested, that he got too angry at my sister. However, my stomach dropped when he followed with, "But spare the rod spoil the child right? Isn't that what the Bible says?" My dad's distortion of how God instructs his children was cruel and self-serving. First, my dad, who hardly ever attended church, was now twisting scripture to justify what he had done. Second, his behavior had placed in me a twisted understanding of what God considers good.

I have grown to love the church. The church, in my understanding, is a group of people learning to be led, not by their own definitions of good, not by their own distortions, or their own impulses, but by the Holy Spirit. It's a group of people who desire to meet together and learn to trust God. It's a group of people who remind each other that though we can *do* good, God *is* good, incapable of evil, and that we are only considered right with God because of Jesus' death on the cross for our sins. It's a group of people encouraging each other to make choices according to God's definition of good—sometimes agreeing with it and sometimes not, sometimes obeying it and sometimes not. In Jesus' language, the church is a group of *disciples*, people learning to trust God, doing things His way. It's a group of people in process, making lots of mistakes, not perfect, but also not content to be who they once were.

The church has become for me a rhythmic weekly and sometimes twice-weekly tradition of relationship with others that encourages my trust, reminding me to *restart* when I need to, and gives me extended opportunities to love and serve others for Jesus. The church is also the place I go to be reminded that I don't need to be the savior of my story. I have a Savior, who asks me to trust that He is God and His sacrifice is enough.

During the hardest seasons with CTD, I needed church to be safe. I needed to know I could walk into the building to learn truths about God's character and attributes, so I had something to anchor to when my human relationships felt untrustworthy. However, some of my hardest days were the days I went to church because many times church was a place where God's attributes were explained incompletely or the sermon contained only part of what the Bible calls *shalom*, leaving me spiraling.

According to Tim Keller in *The Reason for God*,

THE HEBREW WORD *SHALOM* MEANS ABSOLUTE WHOLENESS—FULL, HARMONIOUS, JOYFUL, FLOURISHING LIFE...THE BIBLE DEPICTS A WORLD THAT IS BRIMMING WITH DYNAMIC, ABUNDANT FORMS OF LIFE THAT ARE PERFECTLY INTERWOVEN, INTERDEPENDENT, AND MUTUALLY ENHANCING AND ENRICHING.

*Shalom* is usually translated in English, as *peace*. However, peace simply implies the absence of conflict or the presence of calm. Peace falls short of the full meaning of *shalom*. *Shalom* is interdependent flourishing based on God's definition of good. *Shalom* is a harmonious flourishing with such depth that it is difficult to describe.

Cornelius Plantinga, Jr., in *Not the Way it's Supposed to Be*, suggests a picture of *shalom*:

ABOVE ALL, IN THE VISIONS OF CHRISTIANS AND OTHER THEISTS, GOD WOULD PRESIDE IN THE UNSPEAKABLE BEAUTY FOR WHICH HUMAN BEINGS LONG AND IN THE MYSTERY OF HOLINESS THAT DRAWS HUMAN WORSHIP LIKE A MAGNET. IN TURN, EACH HUMAN BEING WOULD REFLECT AND COLOR THE LIGHT OF GOD'S PRESENCE OUT OF THE INIMITABLE (SO GOOD IT'S IMPOSSIBLE TO COPY) RESOURCES OF HIS OR HER OWN CHARACTER AND ESSENCE. HUMAN COMMUNITIES WOULD PRESENT THEIR ETHNIC AND REGIONAL SPECIALTIES TO OTHER COMMUNITIES IN THE NAME OF GOD, IN GLAD RECOGNITION THAT GOD, TOO, IS A RADIANT AND HOSPITABLE COMMUNITY, OF THREE PERSONS. IN THEIR OWN ACCENTS, COMMUNITIES WOULD EXPRESS PRAISE, COURTESIES, AND DIFFERENCES THAT, WHEN MASSED TOGETHER, WOULD KEEP BUILDING LIKE WAVES OF A PASSION THAT IS NEVER SPENT.

*Shalom* is a state of balance where all living things depend on one another for flourishing and humans are given the distinct role of managing this interdependent flourishing. From the pulpit, presenting a complete message of *shalom*, a state that encompasses all of God's character and attributes and all His ideas of good is imperative for a person with CTD.

The messages I walked into church trying to unlearn were messages about deserving abuse. Messages communicating I was unlovable, that my mistakes caused my dad's anger, that abuse is how God intended for parents to teach their children, that my safety didn't matter, my opinions didn't matter, and my needs didn't matter. While trying to unlearn those messages and make sense of my abuse, an incomplete message about God or His intended state of *shalom* would cause significant confusion for me. I would become triggered and feel angry because of an inconsistency in the message.

For example, the traditional teaching about sin, when addressed outside the framework of *shalom*, would bring up feelings of distrust toward God and the church. Plantinga's definition of sin, "culpable *shalom*-breaking," provides me a healthy framework because it addresses the bigger picture of God's intended purpose for His creation. Plantinga uses the example of murder to illustrate this concept. He asks if murder is a sin if we murder to gain money. He then asks if murder is a sin if we murder to protect our children from being raped, suggesting that killing to protect interdependent flourishing relationships (*shalom*) is not necessarily a sin because the breaking of *shalom* requires reproach. Let me be clear that reproach in the Bible is typically gentle teaching; however, when protecting your children from a heinous crime, gentle teaching may not be suitable to protect what is good.

The trouble with a vague statement like "murder is a sin" is that it falls short of the big picture of the fullness of God and His interdependent flourishing creation, or *shalom*. It reinforces the imbalance and lack of boundaries for a victim.

The psychological deterioration caused by abuse, the confusion regarding boundaries and trust, and the lack of a sense of self, for an abuse victim, result in authority figures (e.g., those at the pulpit) having the final say even if the final say is not a complete message. To help you understand what I mean by this, imagine you adopt two children. One of these children was allowed, while growing up with their biological family, to ask questions, consider options, question authority, and process whether or not they believed something. This child's biological parents trusted in God, praying with the child and living a life God considered good. The other child, while with his biological family was beaten if he had an opinion, questioned anything including authority, or believed anything different from his biological parents. When he was beaten he was told things like "spare the rod, spoil the child" and his sense of self was minimized to absorb the anger of his parents. If these two children walked into church trying to make sense of God while an incomplete message of God was communicated (murder is a sin), which child would walk away asking a question about the message, and which one would walk away angry because they wanted to ask a question, but remembered they'd get a beating for it later?

When God's attributes or definitions of good were preached in part and not in whole, my entire perspective on God would swing like a pendulum. When I was brave enough to ask a question and the question was answered, by people in the church, with seemingly agreed upon, popular church answers rather than personalized answers crafted by the Holy Spirit, again, my entire perspective on God would swing like a pendulum — I would be triggered and walk away keeping my questions to myself. I would feel angry, vulnerable, and completely unsafe. I would assume the trigger was due to God being untrustworthy.

I'm not a pastor, but I have a deep love for several people in my life who are pastors and I know the difficulties of the job and how hard they work. Among a million other tasks, they spend their time loving, supporting, providing counsel, and preaching. Those in their congregations and elsewhere are constantly giving them unsolicited advice. So, to the pastors out there reading this, I am committed to being kind and thoughtful in giving the following, unsolicited advice, from the perspective of an abuse survivor. I hope it will be valuable for you to understand the filter through which abuse victims hear your messages.

So, to you at the pulpit, I know you believe in the broad picture of *shalom*. You believe that the world is not as God wants it to be. You believe He will act to create a different world in which there is this *shalom*. Therefore, my suggestion is to include in your sermons a frequent, simple statement that acknowledges *shalom*. Acknowledging *shalom* will provide boundaries and safety for those in your congregation who have experienced or are experiencing abuse. For example, if you're preaching about God's view on divorce and say, "God hates divorce," don't leave out the *but*. Make a simple statement like, "God hates divorce, *but* He also hates abuse. Abuse in a marriage is an obvious evil, disrupting *shalom*. Therefore, if you have a history of abuse in your marriage or are currently being abused in your marriage, God wants you safe." Then, after explaining how an abuse victim can get help, continue with your sermon. A few simple sentences like these will create safety for a person with CTD so they can stay and listen to why God hates divorce without destroying their trust in God.

Although I won't be cured of CTD, healing from my abuse is vital for truly living. The church and a relationship of trust with God are absolutely essential for healing. And honestly, on my worst days, I needed the church to care for me. In church, I was cared for most by hearing about God in fullness and wholeness so I could spend my days *not* questioning God, but making sense of my abuse and healing from it. I can't tell you how important it was for me to be loved by others on my hard days. However, in the chaos of crisis, in the confusion of abuse, and in the wake of shame, no matter how much love was spoken to me, no matter how much care I was given, I constantly took those messages of human love and care and inserted them into the framework of the love I understood...a love that was self-centered, a love that was confusing and abusive, a love that was not good. In my opinion, the church will spin its wheels trying to love others if the people they are trying to love do not have the framework of *shalom* to place those messages in.

I love this picture of the church painted by Edward T. Welch in *Caring for One Another*:

AS WE COME TO JESUS, HE HAS FORGIVEN AND WASHED US SO THAT WE CAN SPEAK OPENLY WITHOUT SHAME. HE HAS LOVED US SO THAT WE CAN LOVE HIM AND OTHERS FREELY, AND HE HAS GIVEN US WISDOM AND POWER FROM HIS SPIRIT SO THAT WE CAN HELP EACH OTHER IN WAYS THAT BUILD UP AND GIVE HOPE. IN HIS HONOR AND IN HIS STRENGTH WE WANT TO GROW INTO A WONDERFULLY INTERDEPENDENT, WISE, LOVING BODY OF CHRIST-- ONE IN WHICH WE CAN HELP EACH OTHER IN TIMES OF TROUBLE.

If you live with CTD and you find that you're sometimes triggered in church, consider that the trigger might not be God, but an incomplete message of *shalom*. If you find yourself feeling angry by a message that is all grace without truth and boundaries, or all boundaries and truth without love or grace, or all sin without grace, consider that what's triggering you may not be God, *but* an incomplete understanding or message of the fullness of God.

# Ponder

Consider pondering the following questions. To be gentle with yourself, I suggest pondering one set of questions a day, being as honest as possible. Have empathy for yourself in this process.

While listening to a sermon, have you been triggered to the point of feeling angry? List the topics of those sermons.

When considering the sermon topics you listed above, why do you think these topics were triggering? Is it possible the fullness of God or the full message of *Shalom* was not addressed?

Have you ever listened to a sermon that sent you into a tailspin, causing you to question whether or not you should maintain a relationship with your abuser?

Have you ever left church angry? Consider if those moments of anger were the result of a trigger or a vulnerability related to an incomplete message of *shalom*. Is it possible for you to acknowledge that your pastor is human and humans sometimes unintentionally trigger us who have CTD? Is your pastor safe enough to approach with your questions? Are you capable of asking the questions kindly and in a way that doesn't leave you feeling vulnerable?

List the experiences you have had in church where someone else, from their point of view, shared a well- meaning message, a kind word, or set a healthy boundary for themselves, which is part of God's good, but you walked away personally offended, hurt, or triggered. Is it possible that the well-intended actions of the other person were processed through your framework of a love that was not *Good*? Why or why not?

With or without CTD, we all hold distorted views and incomplete messages about God and what He considers good it is important for the people in our churches, including pastors, to consult with and be led by the Holy Spirit. Have you ever asked a question about God and had it answered with a seemingly agreed-upon church statement that didn't reflect the fullness of God? If so, how did you respond?

# Encouragement for the Days Ahead

*To love at all is to be vulnerable. Love anything and your heart will be wrung and possibly broken. If you want to make sure of keeping it intact you must give it to no one, not even an animal. Wrap it carefully round with hobbies and little luxuries; avoid all entanglements. Lock it up safe in the casket or coffin of your selfishness. But in that casket, safe, dark, motionless, airless, it will change. It will not be broken; it will become unbreakable, impenetrable, irredeemable. To love is to be vulnerable. –* CS Lewis

Many years ago I wrote a goal for myself – to one day walk on a road where I don't have to fear the presence of a ravenous beast. This goal won't be met in full until I'm resting with Jesus in heaven. However, it brings me so much joy to tell you I have lots of really good days and nights when even the thought of a ravenous beast is far from my mind. Sometimes I experience multiple days at a time in abandon with a clear sense of self. On my best days, I experience emotion without fear and am present without hypervigilance, allowing me to connect in relationships; allowing my family to thrive.

If you have CTD, no matter the reason why, and are just beginning your journey to understand it, God knows you.

He knows you're exhausted. He knows the world feels unsafe and untrustworthy. He knows things don't always make sense and He knows attachment with others is difficult – there is hope.

I wrote this book to tell you, although your process of healing might be incredibly painful, what owns you now can be managed and used for so much good. The long game will eventually pay off, one day offering you abandon, and joy that eventually leads to *connection* with others.

I hope you experience the presence of the Holy Spirit, I hope you hear you're loved, I hope you can trust someone and find good and healthy ways of managing your nervous system. I'd love to give you a few extra thoughts and encouragement for the days ahead.

1. Move towards the things God considers good.

2. Engage. Stay away from unhealthy things you might use to abandon your life or disengage e.g., drugs, alcohol, sex. I once heard a therapist say, "The opposite of addiction is connection."

3. Keep your vulnerability. If you let your heart become hard to protect yourself, it will be more difficult for you to begin to trust and it will keep you from building amazing relationships.

4. Take every good opportunity given to you. We all need help to grow and succeed in this life. Even those without CTD need help to be successful. It will take courage and vulnerability to

accept help.

5. Let yourself go through the grief cycle. It will come around hundreds of times so accept it and allow yourself to engage with it.

6. Take care of your nervous system (stress response system).

7. Master the restart. When encouraging people to stay on course with their reading of the Bible and their trust in Jesus, my grafted dad, Michael, always says, "Master the restart." I like to apply this to everything in life. I find that it normalizes failure, helping to fight shame.

8. Find your sense of self and set your boundaries.

9. Don't feel sorry for toxic people. Feeling sorry for toxic people will keep you from healing and creating boundaries.

10. Get to know Jesus. If you're at the stage where you want something different from this life but trust no one, I understand where you are and want to remind you that you have a God who is trustworthy and waiting for you to accept His invitation for a relationship. Let Him be your anchor, your shelter, your safe place in this world.

"The LORD bless you and keep you;
the LORD make his face shine on you
and be gracious to you;
the LORD turn his face toward you
and give you peace."
(Numbers 6:24- 26 NIV)

# Thank You

Thank you to BT, BF, CC, DF, JG, JL, MS and LJ at Rosebud Press, for your encouraging words throughout this process, your work in editing and for your cheerleading and reminders of God's truths that helped me finish this work.

Thank you to the numerous people who prayed over this work, and prayed for me during this process.

And most importantly thank you to my husband, who supported me, believing in the importance of this work, and who graciously and lovingly worked to bring beauty and clarity to this book; catching all the dangling participles, adding all the whoms and removing all the thats – because English is hard.

# References

Andrews, Beth. 2011. *Why are you so scared? A Child's Book About Parents With PTSD*. Washington D.C.: Magination Press.

Dennis, Lane T. and Wayne Grudem, eds. 2008. *English Standard Version (ESV) Study Bible*. Wheaton, Illinois: Crossway.

Cloud, Henry, and John Townsend. 1995. *Boundaries Workbook*. Grand Rapids: Zondervan. (35,45,46)

Complextrauma.org

Copan, Paul. 2011. *Is God a Moral Monster? Making Sense of the Old Testament God*. Grand Rapids: Baker Books. (159)

Elwell, Walter A., ed. 1984. *Evangelical Dictionary of Theology*. Grand Rapids: Baker Books. (369, 1196)

Fowler, Bryan, Keith Everette Smith, Micah Darrel Kuiper, and Tasha Layton. *Into The Sea (It's Gonna Be Okay)*

Goff, Bob. 2012. *Love Does*. Nashville: Thomas Nelson. (8)

Grudem, Wayne. 1994. *Systematic Theology: An Introduction to Biblical Doctrine*. Grand Rapids: Zondervan. (187, 490)

Harris, Nadine Burke. 2018. *The Deepest Well*. Boston: Mariner Books. (37, 47-49, 52, 54, 65)

Harrison, Everett, ed. 1971. *The New Testament and Wycliffe Bible Commentary*. Moody Press: Chicago. (264, 1464)

Heard, Matt. 2014. *Life with a Capital L*. Colorado Springs: Multnomah Books. (10-20)

The International Centre for Excellence in Emotionally Focused Therapy (ICEEFT),

Johnson, Sue. 2011. *Hold Me Tight*. London: Piatkus Books. (18-26)

Keller, Timothy. 2018. *The Reason for God: Belief in an Age of Skepticism*. New York: Penguin Books. (50, 176, 177)

Kennedy, Rebecca. 2022. *Good Inside*. New York: Harper Wave. (30)

Mackie, Tim. Podcast.

The National Child Traumatic Stress Network

Packer, J. I. 1993. *Knowing God*. Downers Grove, Illinois: InterVarsity Press. (249)

Pink, Arthur W. 1975. *The Attributes of God*. Grand Rapids: Baker Books. (9, 41, 57-60, 77-81)

Plantinga Jr., Cornelius. 1995. *Not the Way It's Supposed to Be: A Breviary on Sin*. Grand Rapids: Wm. B. Eerdmans Publishing Company. (10, 12, 14, 15, 199)

Purvis, Karyn B., David R. Cross, and Wendy Lyons Sunshine. 2007. *The Connected Child*. New York: McGraw Hill. (48)

Ross, Julia. 2003. *The Mood Cure: The 4-Step Program to Take Charge of Your Emotions Today*. New York: Penguin Random House.

Spangler, Ann. 2004. *Praying the Names of God*. Grand Rapids: Zondervan. (27)

Strobel, Lee. 2009. *The Case for Christ Study Bible. New International Version*. Grand Rapids: Zondervan.

Tracy, Celestia G. 2012. *Mending the Soul Workbook*. Phoenix: Mending the Soul Ministries, Inc. (93)

Welch, Edward T. 2018. *Caring for One Another: 8 Ways to Cultivate Meaningful Relationships*. Wheaton, Illinois: Crossway. (12)

World Health Organization (https://www.who.int/

, https://icd.who.int/browse11/l-m/en#/http%3a%2f%2fid.who.int%2ficd%2fentity%2f585833559)

# About the Author

Evangeline is a writer, photographer, outdoor enthusiast, mother, and wife whose comfort and anchor is Jesus. She is an overcomer and survivor who hopes that her story with Complex Trauma Disorder (CTD) will be an encouragement for others who are navigating their lives and relationships while living with CTD.

For additional resources go to www.evangelinenorth.com.